240 261390

Leukemia

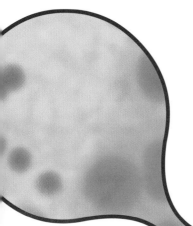

Cancer Genetics

Causes of Cancer

Diagnosis and Treatment of Cancer

Leukemia

Myeloma

Prevention of Cancer

Skin Cancer

Stages of Cancer Development

Testicular Cancer

Leukemia

Donna M. Bozzone Ph.D.

CHELSEA HOUSE
PUBLISHERS
An imprint of Infobase Publishing

THE BIOLOGY OF CANCER: LEUKEMIA

Chelsea House
An imprint of Infobase Publishing
132 West 31st Street
New York NY 10001

Library of Congress Cataloging-in-Publication Data
Bozzone, Donna M.
  Leukemia / Donna M. Bozzone.
    p. cm. — (Biology of cancer)
  Includes bibliographical references and index.
  ISBN-13: 978-0-7910-8822-7 (hardcover : alk. paper)
  ISBN-10: 0-7910-8822-7 (hardcover : alk. paper) 1. Leukemia. I. Title. II. Series.

  RC643.B69 2009
  616.99'419—dc22

                              2008050881

Text design by James Scotto-Lavino
Cover design by Ben Peterson
Illustrations by Chris and Elisa Scherer and Melissa Ericksen

Printed in the United States of America

Bang EJB 10 9 8 7 6 5 4 3 2 1

This book is printed on acid-free paper.

CONTENTS

♦

Foreword 6

1 What Is Leukemia? 11

2 The History of Cancer and Leukemia 23

3 Blood Cell Development and Function 38

4 Leukemias Are Not All the Same 54

5 Childhood Leukemia 71

6 External Risk Factors and Causes of Leukemia 88

7 Internal Responses to Risk Factors: Genes and Chromosome Changes 102

8 Diagnosis, Treatment, and Prevention of Leukemia 116

Notes 135
Glossary 140
Bibliography 149
Further Resources 160
Index 162
About the Author 168

FOREWORD

◆

Approximately 1,500 people die each day of cancer in the United States. Worldwide, more than 8 million new cases are diagnosed each year. In affluent, developed nations such as the United States, around 1 out of 3 people will develop cancer in his or her lifetime. As deaths from infection and malnutrition become less prevalent in developing areas of the world, people live longer and cancer incidence increases to become a leading cause of mortality. Clearly, few people are left untouched by this disease, because of either their own illness or that of loved ones. This situation leaves us with many questions: What causes cancer? Can we prevent it? Is there a cure?

Cancer did not originate in the modern world. Evidence of humans afflicted with cancer dates from ancient times. Examinations of bones from skeletons that are more than 3,000 years old reveal structures that appear to be tumors. Records from ancient Egypt, written more than 4,000 years ago, describe breast cancers. Possible cases of bone tumors have been observed in Egyptian mummies that are more than 5,000 years old. It is even possible that our species' ancestors developed cancer. In 1932 Louis Leakey discovered a jawbone from either *Australopithecus* or *Homo erectus*, which possessed what appeared to be a tumor. Cancer specialists examined the jawbone and suggested that the tumor was due to Burkitt's lymphoma, a type of cancer that affects the immune system.

It is likely that cancer has been a concern for the human lineage for at least a million years.

Human beings have been searching for ways to treat and cure cancer since ancient times, but cancer is becoming an even greater problem today. Because life expectancy increased dramatically in the twentieth century because of public health successes such as improvements in our ability to prevent and fight infectious disease, more people live long enough to develop cancer. Children and young adults can develop cancer, but the chance of developing the disease increases as a person ages. Now that so many people live longer, cancer incidence has increased dramatically in the population. As a consequence, the prevalence of cancer came to the forefront as a public health concern by the middle of the twentieth century. In 1971 President Richard Nixon signed the National Cancer Act and thus declared "war" on cancer. The National Cancer Act brought cancer research to the forefront and provided funding and a mandate to spur research to the National Cancer Institute. During the years since that action, research laboratories have made significant progress toward understanding cancer. Surprisingly, the most dramatic insights came from learning how normal cells function, and by comparing that to what goes wrong in cancer cells.

Many people think of cancer as a single disease, but it actually comprises more than 100 different disorders in normal cell and tissue function. Nevertheless, all cancers have one feature in common: All are diseases of uncontrolled cell division. Under normal circumstances, the body regulates the production of new cells very precisely. In cancer cells, particular defects in deoxyribonucleic acid, or DNA, lead to breakdowns in the cell communication and growth control normal in healthy cells. Having escaped these controls, cancer cells can become invasive and spread to other parts of the body. As a consequence, normal tissue and organ functions may be seriously disrupted. Ultimately cancer can be fatal.

Even though cancer is a serious disease, modern research has provided many reasons to feel hopeful about the future of cancer treatment and prevention. First, scientists have learned a great deal about the specific genes involved in cancer. This information paves the way for improved early detection, such as identifying individuals with a genetic predisposition to cancer and monitoring their health to ensure the earliest possible detection. Second, knowledge of both the specific genes involved in cancer and the proteins made by cancer cells has made it possible to develop very specific and effective treatments for certain cancers. For example, childhood leukemia, once almost certainly fatal, now can be treated successfully in the great majority of cases. Similarly, improved understanding of cancer cell proteins led to the development of new anticancer drugs such as Herceptin, which is used to treat certain types of breast tumors. Third, many cancers are preventable. In fact, it is likely that more than 50 percent of cancers would never occur if people avoided smoking, overexposure to sun, a high-fat diet, and a sedentary lifestyle. People have tremendous power to reduce their chances of developing cancer by making good health and lifestyle decisions. Even if treatments become perfect, prevention is still preferable to avoid the anxiety of a diagnosis and the potential pain of treatment.

The books in the *Biology of Cancer* series reveal information about the causes of the disease; the DNA changes that result in tumor formation; ways to prevent, detect, and treat cancer; and detailed accounts of specific types of cancers that occur in particular tissues or organs. Books in this series describe what happens to cells as they lose growth control and how specific cancers affect the body. *The Biology of Cancer* also provides insights into the studies undertaken, the research experiments done, and the scientists involved in the development of the present state of knowledge of this disease. In this way, readers get to see beyond "the facts" and understand more about the process of biomedical research. Finally, the books in the *Biology of Cancer* series provide information to help readers make healthy choices that can reduce the risk of cancer.

Cancer research is at a very exciting crossroads, affording scientists the challenge of scientific problem solving as well as the opportunity to engage in work that is likely to directly benefit people's health and well-being. I hope that the books in this series will help readers learn about cancer. Even more, I hope that these books will capture your interest and awaken your curiosity about cancer so that you ask questions for which scientists presently have no answers. Perhaps some of your questions will inspire you to follow your own path of discovery. If so, I look forward to your joining the community of scientists; after all, there is still a lot of work to be done.

Donna M. Bozzone, Ph.D.
Professor of Biology
Saint Michael's College
Colchester, Vermont

1
WHAT IS LEUKEMIA?

KEY POINTS

- Cancer is a disease in which cells proliferate without control.

- Cancer is one of the major causes of death in the world.

- Abnormal gene function causes cancer.

- Leukemia is a cancer of blood cells.

- The symptoms of leukemia include fatigue, frequent infections, and easy bruising or bleeding.

- Survival rates for patients with leukemia range from 20 to 90 percent depending upon the specific type of leukemia and the age of the patient.

Neil Keller was a 31-year-old physical education teacher in Frederick, Maryland. He and his wife, Kathy, had two small children; they lived a good and happy life. One day in 1995, Neil experienced a terrible pain in his back. In fact, he was virtually unable to move. His wife noticed that in addition to his back pain, Neil also had a red stripe running down the calf of one of his legs. Kathy took Neil to the emergency room and physicians there explained that the red stripe was due to a blood clot. Additional tests revealed more concerning news—Neil had **leukemia**, a cancer of the blood, and he was in need of immediate attention. **Cancer** is a disease in which cells divide without normal control. In the case of leukemia, an abundance of abnormal blood cells are produced, and as a consequence normal blood cell functions such as carrying oxygen and fighting infection are impaired.

Kathy and Neil left their two small children with their grandparents and Neil was taken to a special cancer hospital in Baltimore, Maryland. The type of leukemia Neil had was **acute lymphocytic leukemia (ALL)**, a disease seen much more commonly in children than adults. At the time of his diagnosis, the number of abnormal leukemia cells in Neil's blood was the highest his doctor had ever seen. Even though Neil was in critical condition, Kathy and the rest of the family had legitimate reason to hope. The physicians explained that ALL had a 90 percent cure rate with a two-year treatment plan.

Unfortunately, Neil was in the 10 percent of the population of ALL patients who were not cured. Although Neil underwent **chemotherapy**, a treatment with drugs to kill the leukemia cells, he did not respond by going into **remission**, a situation in which the cancer cells stop dividing and in many cases actually die. The final effort to save Neil was to do a bone marrow transplant. **Bone marrow** is the soft tissue located in the large bones of the body. The bone marrow is a place where blood cells are made. The idea behind bone marrow transplantation is to provide the leukemia patient with normal blood-making cells so that a renewable population of healthy blood cells can replace the abnormal cells. Neil's *father was the donor for the tissue, but even his generous act could not save his son. Neil died less than a year after he was first diagnosed. It all happened so quickly, and given the initially hopeful predictions regarding Neil's chances, Neil's family and friends were profoundly shocked.*

GENERAL OVERVIEW OF CANCER

One of the major causes of death in the world, cancer is really a set of more than 100 diseases that all have one thing in common: Cells fail to obey the normal controls that the body has to regulate division, **differentiation** or specialization of particular cell types, and cell survival or death. In a healthy body, cells communicate with each other constantly so that they can function together as **tissues**, such as muscle; organs, such as the heart; and organ systems, such as the circulatory system. This carefully orchestrated cell society relies on chemical signals that tell cells to divide, crawl, specialize, or die. These chemical signals are coded for by two categories of genes, **proto-oncogenes** and **tumor suppressors**. **Tumors** are abnormal cell masses, or lumps.

There are hundreds of different proto-oncogenes in all human cells. The **proteins** encoded by the **DNA** of these **genes** include growth factors, **receptors** on cell membranes to which growth factors bind, and molecules inside the cells that pass the information collected at the cell surface to specific areas inside the cell, including the **nucleus**. These proteins encoded by proto-oncogenes comprise a complex regulatory pathway wherein an external signal received by a cell ultimately produces a cellular response. In some cases, the cellular behavior elicited is cell division. Ordinarily, cells proliferate only when told to do so.

Sometimes proto-oncogenes can be altered or mutated so that they no longer function properly. The gene may be changed in such a way that instead of encoding a functional protein, an abnormal protein is produced instead. For example, a receptor for a growth factor that normally triggers cell division when a growth factor binds to it may be altered so that it is permanently stuck "on" even in the absence of a growth factor. The receptor now acts as if the growth factor is bound all the time, even though it is not. Such a cell is going to lack normal control of cell division, attempting to divide even when it has not been told to do so. Proto-oncogenes that undergo **mutations** so that their encoded proteins contribute to cancer development are called **oncogenes**. Oncogenes can be thought of as analogous to a car accelerator in that when they get stuck "on" due to mutations, cell division cannot be easily stopped.

In contrast to proto-oncogenes, tumor suppressor genes encode for proteins that halt cell division, repair DNA damage, and if DNA or cell abnormalities are very serious, trigger cell death. As such, tumor suppressors act like a car's brakes and prevent cell division from getting out of control. When mutations disable tumor suppressor genes, an important mechanism for regulating cell division is lost. Just as having an accelerator stuck "on" will cause a car to accelerate out of control, so too will the loss of brakes prevent stopping it. In the case of cancer, cells need to have more than one active oncogene, and they must lose the functioning of tumor suppressor genes as well in order for a fully **malignant** state to develop. Some tumors, like warts, are **benign**, meaning that they do not continue to grow in an uncontrolled manner and they remain localized where they originated. In contrast, cells of malignant tumors do continue to divide unabated and will spread from their origin by entering the bloodstream and localizing in other tissues in a process called **metastasis**. Cancer can be life threatening because tumors can grow so large that they block circulation or damage normal organ functions. For example, a large lung tumor can crowd out and damage healthy lung tissue, thus seriously impairing breathing.

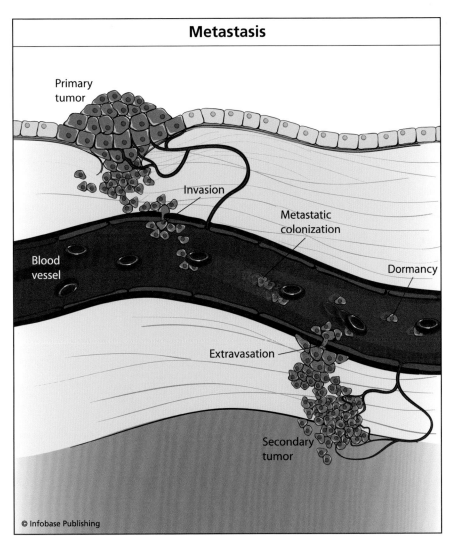

Figure 1.1 Metastasis is the movement of primary cancer cells into the lymphatic and blood systems to secondary sites. After the tumor cells travel to the secondary site (extravasion), the cells will either lie dormant, die, or develop into a secondary cancer.

LEUKEMIA IS A CANCER OF THE BLOOD

Cancer can start in cells of any tissue or organ in the body. Leukemia is different from most other cancers in that it does not produce

♦ THE FLOW OF GENETIC INFORMATION FROM DNA TO PROTEIN

Except for eggs and sperm, each cell of the human body contains 46 **chromosomes** in its nucleus. These 46 chromosomes are actually two sets of 23; one complete set is inherited from the mother, the other set from the father. The chromosomes are composed of DNA and proteins. The genes are inherited instructions of the body that are encoded in the DNA. The proteins associated with chromosomes serve either a structural or regulatory role. Structural proteins help to organize the DNA into well-ordered loops and provide a physical scaffold for the chromosome. Regulatory proteins generally help to determine which genes are turned "on" and which are "off."

The genetic information present in DNA is a consequence of its chemical structure. DNA is composed of several types of chemical building blocks. The sugar, deoxyribose, and phosphate hook together to make a ribbon-like backbone. Four types of bases containing nitrogen, abbreviated A, G, T, C, connect to the sugars of the backbone. These bases stick out from the molecule like little flat plates. The language of DNA is the order of these bases. Specific sequences of bases direct the cell to make a particular type of protein. Just as the identity and arrangement of letters in words indicate meaning—took versus tool versus loot, for example—the identity and arrangement of bases provide information to the cell.

solid masses or tumors. Because leukemia is a consequence of the uncontrolled division of certain types of blood cells, these cancer cells can proliferate within the circulatory system. And since no growths or lumps are evident, it can be initially challenging to realize that the disease is present.

Symptoms and Diagnosis

While many of the early symptoms of leukemia are noticeable, they are sufficiently general that a person might not become especially concerned. After all, there are many reasons one might experience fatigue, headaches, fever, chills, or a general lack of "well-being." As the disease progresses, however, the signs become more difficult to ignore: night sweats, easy bruising and bleeding, swollen gums, frequent infections, swollen lymph nodes, shortness of breath, and weight loss. Eventually, symptoms can become quite concerning: joint pain, bone pain, and abdominal swelling.

Leukemia is usually detected because a person experiencing one or more of the symptoms detailed above visits his or her physician and is carefully examined. The doctor will examine the patient to see if there is abdominal swelling or tenderness as might be expected if the **spleen**, a blood-forming organ, was enlarged. Blood tests will also be performed to see whether blood cells are present in healthy numbers and to determine if abnormal blood cells are evident. Many of the physical symptoms of leukemia derive from the loss of normal blood cells. For example, because red blood cells carry oxygen in the blood, an inadequate supply of these cells renders a person **anemic** and quite fatigued. White blood cells are responsible for fighting infection, so when they are not functioning, a person gets sick more often. Finally, leukemia can disrupt the production of **platelets**, cell fragments responsible for blood clotting. A reduction of these blood components causes a person to bruise and bleed easily.

In addition to a physical examination and blood tests, doctors may evaluate patients by examining bone marrow to see what might be wrong with blood cell development. A technique called **cytogenetics**, allows technicians to stain the chromosomes of the leukemia cells with dyes so they can examine them microscopically in order to see whether they

SPOTLIGHT ON CANCER SCIENTISTS
JOHN HUGHES BENNETT, M.D. (1812–1875)

In 1845 Dr. John Hughes Bennett published a celebrated paper entitled "Case of Hypertrophy of the Spleen and Liver, in Which Death Took Place From Suppuration of the Blood," in which he and his colleague, Dr. David Craigie, recorded two of the first clinical descriptions of leukemia. This contribution to medicine was only one of many that Dr. Bennett made over the course of his eminent career.

Born in 1812 in London, England, Bennett came from a cultured and intellectual household. He was educated at Exeter, a rigorous private school, where he was trained in elocution and read Shakespeare aloud from an early age; as an adult, Bennett was a famously talented speaker who expressed himself in an elegant and dramatic style. He began his medical education in 1829 as an apprentice to the surgeon, Mr. Sedgwick. Early on, Bennett became interested in **pathology**, the study of disease, and assisted Sedgwick in many **autopsies**. In fact, Bennett's enthusiasm got the best of him, and he and another student performed an autopsy without permission. Mr. Sedgwick found out and immediately dismissed Bennett.

are damaged and if so, the specific nature of the damage. Molecular techniques may also be used to determine whether the DNA sequence of proto-oncogenes or tumor suppressors has been affected. Various diagnostic techniques are used in order to determine precisely what type of leukemia is present so that effective treatments can be attempted.

After worrying that he had ruined his future, in 1833 Bennett had the opportunity to resume his medical studies at the University of Edinburgh in Scotland. He was very successful: He published two papers while still a student and earned an M.D. with highest honors and a gold medal in 1837. Bennett continued his medical studies in France and Germany. He learned how to use microscopy in medical practice and for medical instruction. Bennett returned to Edinburgh in 1841, determined to reform aspects of clinical practice and education.

Bennett's career in Edinburgh was very productive. He was the first person to teach **histology**, the systematic study of cells and tissues using a microscope. He also recognized the importance of examining diseased organs and tissues with microscopy so that pathologies could be observed. He worked hard to modernize medicine, arguing against **bloodletting** and the overly high does of medicines prescribed to some patients. It was also in Edinburgh that Bennett observed and described leukemia.

As a person, Bennett was highly respected, but because he had a sharp tongue, some people were frightened by him and did not like him. However, underneath his somewhat gruff exterior was a kind person. Bennett was beloved by those who were close to him, and affection for him grew deeper the longer a person knew him.

HOW COMMON IS LEUKEMIA AND CAN PEOPLE SURVIVE?

Approximately 200,000 people in the United States are living with leukemia. Each year, 35,000 new cases are diagnosed. In 1960, only 14 percent of people with leukemia survived for five years. Since then, survival has increased to approximately 50 percent overall, thanks to the development of new treatments and therapies. However, there are several forms of leukemia, and the survival rates range from 20 to 90 percent depending on the specific type of leukemia and the age of the patient.[1]

Although leukemia is 10 times more prevalent in adults than in children, it accounts for more than 30 percent of all childhood cancers.

◆ BLOOD IS LIFE

From earliest recorded history, humans have recognized the fundamental importance of blood even if they did not understand exactly how blood functioned in the body. Blood was characterized as the body's source of nourishment, and physicians in ancient times thought that "disordered" blood produced fever and illness. The ancient Greeks thought that health depended on a harmonious balance of all the body's fluids, and that certain physical problems, such as headache or fever, were caused by a buildup of too much blood. The remedy for this problem was bloodletting, or the removal of "excess" blood. This medical technique persisted well into the nineteenth century even though it was not effective for curing disease. In fact, overly enthusiastic bloodletting sometimes caused serious harm. In 1799, George Washington complained of a sore throat. When three of the

In fact, leukemia affects approximately 2,200 children per year in the United States. The age at which a person develops leukemia depends on the specific type of the disease and can occur in infancy or in later years. More than 50 percent of leukemia cases are in people older than 64 years.[2]

For reasons that are not understood, leukemia **incidence** varies in different populations. For example, 57 percent of all cases are seen in males and only 43 percent in females. (In addition, the death rate of leukemia is 27 percent higher in men than in women: Of the 22,280 people who died of leukemia in 2006, 12,470 were male and 9,810 were

most respected physicians of the day came to heal the former president, they bled Washington until he died 48 hours later.

In addition to understanding that blood is necessary for the life of the body, people have also connected it with things that have no relation to biology. For example, blood is used figuratively and literally in the religious rituals of many faith traditions, charms, and fertility rites. Strength, courage, and youth were thought to reside in the blood. This idea was so strong that during the Renaissance the physicians of Pope Innocent VII are said to have prescribed human blood to save the dying pope. This treatment was not effective: The pope as well as his three young blood donors died.

Our fascination and relationship with blood are not relics of the past. We hold "blood drives" to collect blood from volunteers so that sick people can be helped. Many people practice religions in which blood is an important symbol. And a trip to a movie theater will usually offer at least one entertainment choice that will be awash in blood.

female.) Leukemia incidence is also highest in Caucasians and lowest in Native Americans and Alaskan natives. Leukemia rates are higher for white and Latino children and lowest in African-American children. In fact, Latinos under the age of 20 years have the highest rate of leukemia.[3] It is likely that differences in leukemia among these groups offer clues about the cause and development of this disease. Scientists are working hard to try to solve this important puzzle.

SUMMARY

Cancer, a disease in which the normal controls that regulate cell division do not operate properly, can affect people at any age. The basis for the loss of growth control is a malfunction of specific genes. Leukemia is a particular type of cancer that causes the uncontrolled **proliferation** of abnormal blood cells. Because the abnormal cells crowd out the normal blood cells, a person suffering from leukemia may experience a range of symptoms including fatigue, infections, bruising, bleeding, and headaches. Although some other forms of cancer are more common, approximately 200,000 people in the United States have leukemia and 35,000 new cases are diagnosed each year. The rate of survival depends on the type of leukemia and the age of the patient.

2

THE HISTORY OF CANCER AND LEUKEMIA

KEY POINTS

♦ Cancer has affected humans since the beginning of our existence as a species.

♦ Cancer is found in species besides humans.

♦ Before scientists understood that cells are the building blocks of living organisms, they thought cancer was caused by an imbalance of body fluids.

♦ In the nineteenth century, scientists recognized that cancer is a cellular disease.

♦ Scientists also discovered that some cancers can be attributed to external causes such as smoking, exposure to high-energy radiation, or exposure to certain chemicals.

♦ Leukemia was first described as a blood cell cancer in the mid-nineteenth century.

CANCER IS OLDER THAN PEOPLE

In 1932, the anthropologist Louis Leakey uncovered an amazing fossil in Kenya. It was the jaw of an ancient ancestor of humans. Although it was exciting to find bones of pre-human hominids, there was something even more special about this particular specimen. The jawbone exhibited a distinctive swelling that appeared to be the result of a malignant tumor. While no one can be completely certain that a lump on a fossilized bone was caused by a malignant tumor, it is interesting to note that Burkitt's lymphoma, a type of cancer found today in East Africa, produces jaw tumors. It is extremely likely that cancer was a health problem for organisms long before modern humans evolved. In fact, cancers can develop in all types of vertebrates, as well as in mollusks and other invertebrates, and even in plants.

CANCER THROUGHOUT HISTORY

In addition to Leakey's tantalizing discovery of a fossilized tumor, ancient human remains have also revealed evidence of cancer. For example, bone tumors and possible **nasopharyngeal** cancers have been observed in some Egyptian mummies from 5000 B.C.E. Similarly, mummified skeletal remains of the Incas, found in Peru and dating back to 2400 BCE, have lesions characteristic of metastatic **melanoma**, a form of skin cancer. In another case, lesions found in the skull of a woman from the Bronze Age (1900–1600 B.C.E) are consistent with those that occur in metastatic breast cancer or melanoma.[1]

Because cancer has always been an aspect of the human experience, it is described throughout recorded history, including detailed theories of cancer's causes as well as efforts to treat the disease. The first recorded description of tumors and their treatments is in the Ramayana, a text from ancient India (circa 2000 B.C.E); the treatments included cutting out tumors surgically or applying healing ointments containing arsenic. The ancient Egyptians also treated superficial skin cancers with caustic arsenic pastes. Their written records (from around 1500 B.C.E.) also refer to breast cancers and a treatment called the "fire drill," in which cancerous tissue was cauterized or burned in order to destroy it.

The ancient Greeks were the first civilization to recognize cancer as a distinct disease. It is from them that we get the term **carcinoma**, meaning crab. The Greeks coined the term carcinoma because they thought that the finger-like projections spreading from a tumor looked like a crab. Hippocrates (460–370 BCE), often characterized as the "father of medicine," made important observations about cancer. Hippocrates described cancers of the breast, stomach, skin, **cervix**, **rectum**, and nasopharynx. He also developed guidelines for treatment. He proposed surgical removal of accessible tumors and treatment of the wound created by the surgery with ointments containing herbal poisons such as hemlock, belladonna, or arsenic. These poisons were believed to be able to kill any remaining bits of tumor that the surgery did not remove. Hippocrates also advised that no operations should be performed on patients with internal tumors, because surgery and its complications would likely cause the patient to die sooner than would the tumor.

Whereas Hippocrates may be called the father of medicine, Galen, a Greek physician who lived in Rome during the second century A.D., is regarded by many as the first **oncologist**, or cancer specialist. Among his many responsibilities, Galen was the physician for the Roman gladiators. As a consequence of tending to wounded fighters, Galen developed great expertise in human anatomy. He also recorded detailed descriptions of various organs such as the intestines, the female reproductive

Figure 2.1   Galen lived from 131 until 231 C.E. *(U.S. National Library of Medicine/National Institutes of Health)*

tract, and the breasts. Galen's advice regarding treatment and surgery agreed exactly with that of Hippocrates.

Even though the descriptions of cancers in those ancient records were quite detailed, no one understood how cancers formed and spread. From the time of the ancient Greeks until the 1860s, people believed that cancers were caused by the accumulation of amorphous or formless liquids in various parts of the body. Physicians thought that these liquids would accumulate in parts of the body that were injured or overused. These ideas regarding how cancer developed led to some treatments that seem useless or even bizarre to us today. For example, in addition to surgery, doctors also lanced swellings or suspicious areas and/or removed blood. Both lancing and bloodletting were done to remove these "bad liquids" from the body. Even more bizarre, reports from the 1600s detail treating ulcerous carcinomas with the extracts of puppies boiled in wine and curing breast cancer by attaching eight frogs at a time to the affected breast and letting them suck the fluids like leeches.

By the 1600s, scientists observed that the body was composed of tissues that were made of various amorphous materials and different types of fibers. They recognized and named **epithelial**, muscular, neural, and connective tissues. With no knowledge of cells as the basic building blocks of all living things, scientists continued to think that metastasis, or the spreading of cancer, was due to the traveling of a "bad" fluid to distant parts of the body.

The development of the cell theory in the mid-1800s triggered a complete reconceptualization of science. Rudolf Virchow, a German physician and scientist, stated it clearly: "*Omnis cellula a cellula,*" meaning that every cell comes from the reproduction of other cells. Cells and tissues do not form from amorphous liquids and neither do tumors.

(continues on page 32)

◆ MEDICINAL LEECHES:
A NEW USE FOR AN ANCIENT TREATMENT

Leeches have been used for thousands of years to remove blood from patients in an effort to treat a wide range of ailments. More than 5,000 years ago, Egyptian physicians thought that leeches could cure many ailments including fevers and flatulence. In ancient India, bloodletting was done to treat illness, and leeching was considered to be the most precise method because of the reputed ability of leeches to distinguish between "good" and "bad" blood.

Bleeding patients with leeches was not limited to ancient times. In fact, well into the nineteenth century, apothecary shops (pharmacies) stocked live leeches. The height of medicinal use was in the mid-1800s. By that time, physicians in Paris, France, used millions of leeches per year. Eventually, when medicinal leeches became endangered in Western Europe it became necessary to import them. By the end of the nineteenth century, medical use of leeches fell out of favor as other medical techniques were developed and improved.

This semi-retirement of leeches ended in 1985 with a breakthrough in microsurgery. A surgeon was trying to reattach an ear to a five-year-old patient, but the tiny veins kept clotting. Reasoning that leeches can stop blood clotting because of the chemical **hirudin** in their blood, the surgeon attached leeches around the wound. He knew that pooled blood around a wound endangers tissue survival. The attached leeches promoted blood flow to the area, removed excess blood, and ensured that an appropriate

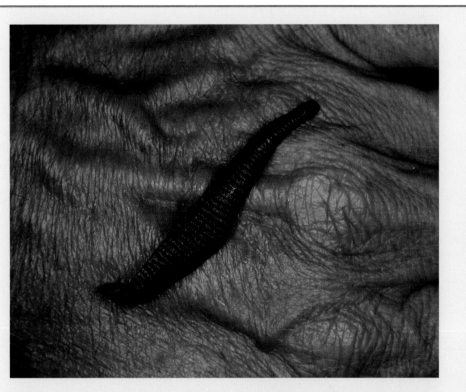

Figure 2.2   Today, medicinal leeches are used to help speed the healing of skin grafts and finger reattachments. *(© Bill Beatty/Visuals Unlimited)*

amount of oxygenated blood was always present near the wound. As a consequence, the tiny veins had the opportunity to regenerate and reconnect circulation. The ear was saved.[2]

Leeches have proven effective in healing skin grafts and aiding plastic or reconstructive surgery including reattachment of fingers. In 2004, the Food and Drug Administration (FDA) cleared the first application for medicinal leeches, *Hirudo medicinalis*, to be used as medical devices.

SPOTLIGHT ON CANCER SCIENTISTS:

GIOVANNI BATTISTA MORGAGNI, M.D., PH.D.
(1682–1771)

Imagine waking up in the middle of the night with an intense pain on the right side of your lower abdomen. Maybe you are running a fever and feel nauseous. Because the pain is difficult to tolerate, you decide to go to the emergency room for medical attention. Once you arrive, physicians examine you and, based on the symptoms you are presenting, they think you might be suffering from appendicitis. They conduct additional tests to verify this diagnosis. If it turns out to be correct, the treatment will be surgery to remove the inflamed appendix. Because you are in good health generally, your prognosis is excellent. You will recover fully.

How is it that physicians can make accurate diagnoses from a physical examination of the body? The symptoms of appendicitis displayed by someone during the Middle Ages probably would have elicited a diagnosis that the individual was possessed by an evil

Figure 2.3 Giovanni Battista Morgagni. *(U.S. National Library of Medicine/National Institutes of Health).*

sprit or that the bodily fluids were not "balanced." In either case, the treatment would be bloodletting and if the appendix ruptured, the patient would die. It is thanks to Italian physician and scientist Giovanni Battista Morgagni that we no longer take such an ineffective and potentially dangerous approach to diagnosis and treatment.

Born in 1682, Morgagni revealed his scholarly talent even as a boy. He started his medical studies in Bologna, Italy, in 1698. By 1701 Morgagni had earned his M.D. and Ph.D.: he was only 19 years old. He decided to become an anatomist and devoted himself to pathology. Morgagni's undeniable ability enabled him to advance into professional positions of increasing responsibility and eminence. By 1715 he was named Chair of Anatomy at the University of Padua, where he remained for the rest of his life.

Morgagni was an excellent teacher and a prolific writer. Among his many important findings and discoveries, the most influential was his concept that the diagnosis, treatment, and prognosis of disease depend on knowing the pathological changes in anatomy. In 1761 he published his masterpiece, *Seats and Causes of Disease Investigated by Means of Anatomy*, a five-volume work that is the foundation for modern pathological anatomy. In this treatise, Morgagni describes the observations and findings he made in 640 autopsies. He is the first person ever to connect what he saw in the cadaver to clinical findings for that individual. Morgagni insisted that physicians needed to think of disease in terms of localized pathologies rather than body fluid imbalances. Thanks to him, physicians and scientists turned their attentions to developing new tools, methods, and techniques that could reveal hidden anatomical pathologies in living patients.

(continued from page 27)

Cancer cells are produced by other cells, and metastasis is due to the migration of these cells to other parts of the body.

By the late 1860s scientists were able to do careful microscopic studies of cells and tumors in order to learn more about cancer. In 1869 Wilhelm Waldeyer, a German scientist, published a paper in which he detailed the pathology of breast cancer. He presented evidence that the tumor was

SPOTLIGHT ON CANCER SCIENTISTS:
RUDOLF VIRCHOW, M.D. (1821–1902)

Aspects of our understanding of the cellular basis for many diseases, including cancer, derive from the pioneering work of the German **pathologist** and physician, Rudolf Virchow. Born in 1821 to a family of modest financial means, Virchow's early education revealed his great promise. As a consequence, he received free medical training in Berlin, Germany. Virchow began his medical studies in 1839 and received his M.D. in 1843. Particularly fascinated by pathological histology, the study of diseased cells and tissues, Virchow published a paper in 1845 that contained one of the earliest pathological descriptions of leukemia.

In addition to his scientific and medical work, Virchow was an ardent social reformer. For example, in 1848 he was appointed by the government to investigate an outbreak of typhus fever in the country. Virchow's report blamed social conditions and the government for the state of affairs that led to the outbreak. Virchow noted that improperly functioning sewers, a lack of clean drinking water, and crowded conditions were instrumental in the spread of the disease. Not only did

epithelial in nature and had in fact arisen from normal epithelial tissue. Moreover, he observed that the tumor spread into the local area and then to distant sites due to tumor cells that had entered the bloodstream and were carried elsewhere. Waldeyer even observed that cancer cells could stimulate the growth of **capillaries**, or small blood vessels, which would connect to the tumor and bring it blood to support its growth. This paper was astonishing in its detail and accuracy; it still holds up today.

government officials ignore his recommendations for alleviating these problems, but they also suspended Virchow for two weeks and then reinstated him in a demoted position. Nevertheless, Virchow stayed active in his reform efforts, all the while treating patients and doing scientific research. In 1856 a chair of pathological anatomy was established for Virchow in Berlin—in fact, an entire pathological institute was built for him at the University of Berlin. Virchow worked there for the rest of his life.

Among Virchow's many accomplishments was his recognition that outside stimuli affected cells, and that diseased cells come from already diseased cells. He realized that all cells arise from other cells, including cancer cells. Also, he understood that cancer cells came from previously healthy cells. In his research, Virchow emphasized clinical observation, physiological experiments using laboratory animals, and pathological anatomy especially at the microscopic level. In 1858 Virchow published one of the most important books in modern medicine, *Cellular Pathology as Based Upon Physiological and Pathological Histology*. With this publication, Virchow firmly established that the cell was the most important aspect of disease pathologies, including cancer.

IDEAS ABOUT CAUSES

It took thousands of years for scientists and doctors to observe and describe the cellular events that occur in cancer. Similarly, it has taken a long time to understand something about the potential causes of cancer. From ancient times to the twentieth century, cancer has been attributed to causes that include evil spirits and demons, emotional turmoil, tight clothing, and physical injury. The problem was so serious that doctors entertained all ideas in hope of preventing and curing this disease. However, by the time of the Renaissance, people began to suspect correctly that certain human activities increased the likelihood of cancer. In 1604, King James I of England's *A Counterblaste to Tobacco* described the evils of smoking and the health problems it produced. He even encouraged the public display of lungs blackened by tobacco smoke. In 1761 John Hill, an English physician, warned that inhaling snuff, finely ground tobacco, caused nasal cancer. The relationship between exposure to chimney soot in chimney sweeps and the development of **scrotal** cancer in these individuals was well documented by the English surgeon Percival Potts in 1775. This was the first example of a cancer caused by a workplace exposure to a **carcinogen**, or cancer-causing material. Other potential workplace carcinogens include **X-rays**, asbestos fibers, certain chemical solvents, and **radioactive** dust from mining.

In addition to occupational cancers, other patterns of cancer related to human activity were discovered. For example, a medical study done in Chicago in 1907 showed that cancer rates were higher in meat-eaters—individuals of German, Irish, or Scandinavian origins—than in pasta- or rice-eaters—people originally from Italy or China. Scientists also observed that specific cancer incidences varied geographically. For example, breast cancer rates are higher in North America and Western Europe than in Japan, where the rates of stomach cancer are greater. These differences in cancer incidence are likely due to differences in diet and lifestyle. Perhaps the most startling example of a human behavior related to cancer is that of tobacco smoking. Cigarette smokers have a dramatically higher incidence of lung and other forms of cancer than do nonsmokers. The likelihood of developing a smoking-related cancer increases the longer and the greater the number of cigarettes one smokes.

Finally, scientists explored the possibility that cancer was caused by an infection. Although there are some **viruses**, bacteria, and even flatworms that can cause certain human cancers, in developed countries such as the United States, only approximately 5 percent of cancers can be attributed to infection. In stark contrast, more than 20 percent of cancers detected in people in developing countries are caused in this way.[3]

HISTORY OF LEUKEMIA

Because leukemia is a type of cancer that develops from blood-forming cells, it does not produce a solid tumor. As consequence, it was difficult for doctors and scientists to recognize that leukemia was actually a malignant cancer.

In 1827, the French physician Velpeau described what he observed in the autopsied body of a man who had complained of fever, weakness, headaches, and other pains. Velpeau weighed the deceased man's enlarged spleen; it was 10 pounds. A normal spleen weighs less than one-half of a pound. Also, the man's blood was filled with white material that Velpeau identified as pus. In 1839, two other French physicians described similar cases in which the deceased individuals had complained of fever and weakness. They also had enlarged spleens and white material in their blood. These physicians did not think this white material was pus but suggested that it was comprised of white blood cells.

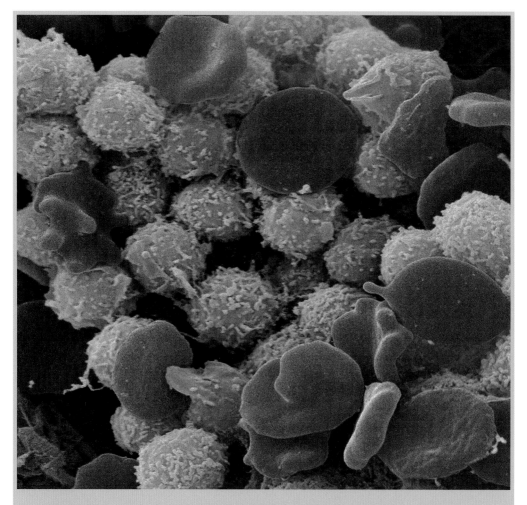

Figure 2.4   This colored scanning electron micrograph (SEM) shows a blood sample from a person with chronic lymphocytic leukemia (CLL). The sample contains a far greater number of white blood cells (blue) than would a sample from a healthy person.

In 1845 three physicians and scientists independently determined the correct nature of the white material in the blood, although they did not understand that they were observing a type of cancer. In Edinburgh,

Scotland, Dr. John Bennett autopsied a man whose spleen was enlarged to more than seven pounds. Bennett examined the man's blood microscopically and observed an abundance of white blood cells. Similarly, Dr. Craigie, also in Edinburgh, autopsied a man possessing a nearly eight-pound spleen. A direct examination of his blood also revealed an abundance of white blood cells. Finally, based on a closer, direct observation of blood, Rudolf Virchow in Germany identified "weisse Blut," what we call leukemia—an imbalance between white blood cells and red blood cells.

Because leukemia was not recognized as a cancer until the mid–nineteenth century, older ideas about causes, treatments, and cures for this specific disease really do not exist. Once people understood that leukemia was a blood cancer, a great deal of thinking, research, and effort was devoted to improving diagnosis, treatment, and prevention.

SUMMARY

Cancer is not a modern phenomenon; it has been a health concern since the dawn of humanity. Ancient records from Egypt, India, Greece, and Rome describe the existence of various forms of cancer as well as efforts to treat the disease and understand its causes. Leukemia, a cancer of blood cells, was more difficult to recognize because solid tumors or lumps do not generally form. The clinical description of leukemia was not recorded until the mid–nineteenth century. Physicians really had no idea how to treat the disease until many years later.

3

BLOOD CELL DEVELOPMENT AND FUNCTION

KEY POINTS

♦ Blood consists of blood cells suspended in a liquid called plasma.

♦ The major components of the blood cell population are erythrocytes (red blood cells), leukocytes (white blood cells), and platelets.

♦ There are many types of leukocytes, each performing different functions.

♦ Blood cells originate from a self-renewing population of stem cells.

♦ Leukemia symptoms result from the inability of blood cells to perform their normal functions in the body.

Tom Kochanowicz, a 38-year-old man from Omaha, Nebraska, went to see his family physician for a checkup. Tom was feeling tired and he had been getting colds more frequently. Also, he had noticed that if he cut himself shaving, it took a little longer than usual for the bleeding to stop. At the time of this checkup the doctor detected a worrisome lump in Tom's side—perhaps an enlarged spleen or lymph node. Additional tests revealed that Tom was suffering from a slow-growing form of leukemia. The abnormal cells were gradually overwhelming the normal cells in his blood. An inadequate number of normal cells were able to form. As a consequence, Tom experienced a variety of symptoms, each of which could be attributed to the failure or depletion of particular types of blood cells.

HOW DO BLOOD CELLS FORM AND DEVELOP?

Blood is actually a type of tissue in which the different types of cells work together to perform specific functions but are not physically connected. In fact, blood cells are suspended in a complex liquid called **plasma**. In a sample of blood, 55 percent of blood volume is plasma and 45 percent is composed of cells. The plasma itself is 90 percent water with the remaining 10 percent containing materials such as oxygen, carbon dioxide, nutrients, hormones, waste products of metabolism, proteins important for blood clotting and immune responses, and electrolytes needed for water balance and cell membrane function. The blood cell population also has several different components: **erythrocytes**, or red blood cells; **leukocytes**, or white blood cells; and platelets.

Unlike some cells, such as muscle or brain cells, blood cells do not live for long time periods. For example, erythrocytes have a lifespan of 120 days and leukocytes live from hours to weeks, depending upon the specific type of leukocyte. Once cells have worn out, they die, the useful components of the resulting debris are recycled, and waste products

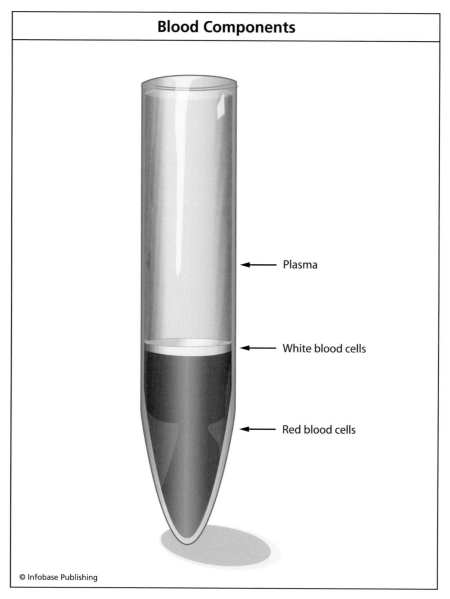

Blood Components

Figure 3.1   The main components of blood are plasma, leukocytes and platelets, and erythrocytes. Plasma, the most abundant component, makes up about 55 percent of blood's volume. Erythrocytes make up about 45 percent of blood's volume. Leukocytes and platelets make up less than 1 percent of blood's volume.

are eliminated from the body. Because the body makes new blood cells continuously throughout a person's life, old and damaged blood cells are easily replaced.

Blood cells form and develop in the bone marrow, the spongy material found inside bones. All blood cells, no matter what type, originate from **pluripotent** stem cells, which are located in the marrow. Pluripotent means that these cells are not fully specialized or differentiated. In fact, they can undergo cell division and make cells that can ultimately form different types of blood cells, depending on the instructions received from other cells, their local tissue environment, and the body. For example, when a person is ill with an infection, the body sends a signal to the bone marrow that directs the **stem cells** to make leukocytes, which help fight the infection. This blood production factory works throughout a person's life because in addition to producing offspring that will ultimately become blood cells, stem cells can also make new stem cells, thus replenishing the supply of their own population.

A closer look at how blood cells form reveals a complicated picture. The process of blood cell formation is called **hematopoiesis**. All blood cells do indeed originate from a pluripotent stem cell. When a pluripotent stem cell divides, the resulting cells can be another pluripotent stem cell, or a **lymphoid** stem cell, or a **myeloid** stem cell. Lymphoid and myeloid refer to two different lineages or branches of the blood cell "family tree." Let's follow the specific pathways of the myeloid and lymphoid lineages.

Myeloid stem cells are located in the bone marrow. The types of cells that are made from this line include erythrocytes, **megakaryo-cytes** (these produce platelets and are important for blood clotting), and five types of leukocytes: **basophils, eosinophils, neutrophils,**

Hematopoiesis

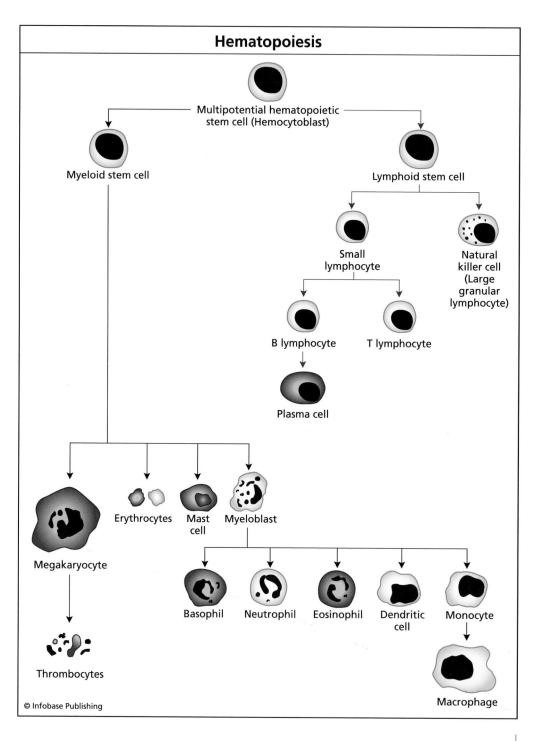

Multipotential hematopoietic
stem cell (Hemocytoblast)

Myeloid stem cell

Lymphoid stem cell

Small
lymphocyte

Natural
killer cell
(Large
granular
lymphocyte)

B lymphocyte   T lymphocyte

Plasma cell

Megakaryocyte

Erythrocytes   Mast
cell

Myeloblast

Basophil   Neutrophil   Eosinophil   Dendritic
cell

Monocyte

Thrombocytes

Macrophage

dendritic cells, and **monocytes** (these become **macrophages**, which are important for removing bacteria and dirt.)

Lymphoid stem cells are also located in the bone marrow. These cells can produce three types of leukocytes: **NK** or **natural killer cells**, **B lymphocytes**, and **T lymphocytes**. All of the leukocytes fight infection in ways specific to their cell type.

FUNCTIONS OF HEALTHY BLOOD CELLS AND THE IMPACT OF LEUKEMIA

Numbering between 5 and 6 million per milliliter of blood, erythrocytes are by far the most abundant type of blood cells. This means that our body contains approximately 5 trillion erythrocytes in the five liters of blood each of us possesses! The principal job of red blood cells is to transport oxygen. In fact, each erythrocyte contains 250 million molecules of the oxygen-binding protein, **hemoglobin**. Because each hemoglobin molecule can carry four oxygen molecules, each red blood cell can transport up to 1 billion oxygen molecules.[1] Thus oxygen, carried by the erythrocytes, is delivered to every organ and cell in the body.

Oxygen is essential for the functioning and survival of all cells and organs. It is also important for the body to have adequate oxygen so that sufficient energy will be available to power physical exertion. Exercising, running, or doing anything that is physically demanding increases the breathing rate, which allows more oxygen to reach muscles and organs. A person with leukemia may tire or fatigue easily if the abnormal cells are outnumbering normal erythrocytes. When healthy erythrocytes are in short supply, oxygen delivery can be greatly diminished.

Figure 3.2 *(opposite page)* This diagram shows the process of the formation and differentiation of stem cells, called hematopoiesis.

Next in order of relative abundance in the blood are platelets; one milliliter of blood contains 250,000 to 300,000 of these cellular elements. Platelets are not exactly cells. They are produced by huge cells, mega-karyocytes, which are from the myeloid lineage. Megakaryocytes shed small, very short-lived fragments. These fragments, or platelets, live only 5 to 9 days. They are located throughout tissues of the body and are

SPOTLIGHT ON CANCER SCIENTISTS:
PAUL EHRLICH, M.D. (1854–1915)

Although trained as a physician, Paul Ehrlich preferred medical research to clinical practice. A sensitive, modest, and somewhat timid man, Ehrlich did not want to witness the suffering of patients or to inflict pain treating them. Nevertheless, the accomplishments of his life's work helped an enormous number of patients in his day and built the foundation for breakthroughs that ease sickness today.

Born in Germany in 1854, Ehrlich earned his M.D. in 1878. He published a remarkable thesis that described his pioneering methods for staining animal cells and tissues with colored dyes, thus making previously invisible structures easy to see with a microscope. Ehrlich continued this work and ultimately developed methods to stain blood cells so that all types could be identified. This work was essential for all future research in hematology, histology, immunology, and oncology.

In addition to this area of research, Ehrlich also tackled two other problems that are significant to our understanding of leukemia and the treatment of disease. After his cell-staining studies, Ehrlich turned his

essential for blood clotting. When platelets are in short supply due to leukemia, cuts bleed for longer time periods, bruises occur more readily, and when bruises do happen, they are larger because the internal bleeding that causes bruising can persist.

Finally, the least numerous but certainly not least important blood cells are leukocytes, or white blood cells. One milliliter of blood contains

attention to the function of the leukocytes, or white blood cells. In 1891 he discovered that when he exposed mice to plant poisons such as ricin or abrin, the mice produced antibodies in their blood. These antibodies rendered the mice resistant to the poison. Ehrlich called this phenomenon **immunization**; he was awarded the Nobel Prize in 1908 for his "side-chain theory" of antibody formation.

Ehrlich also founded the field of chemotherapy. He reasoned that chemicals could be developed that would attack infectious organisms specifically without harming the host. Ehrlich succeeded in developing a treatment for syphilis, a sexually transmitted disease that had long been a scourge on society. Ehrlich's ideas about chemotherapy have been adapted effectively to develop drugs for other types of infectious disease, as well as cancer in general and leukemia in particular.

Ehrlich was a very energetic and careful experimentalist who enjoyed the affection and respect of all who worked with him. He was kind and devoted to his wife and two daughters. Perhaps the only complaint anyone ever had about him concerned his lifelong habit of smoking 25 strong cigars each day. He died in 1915 after suffering a stroke.

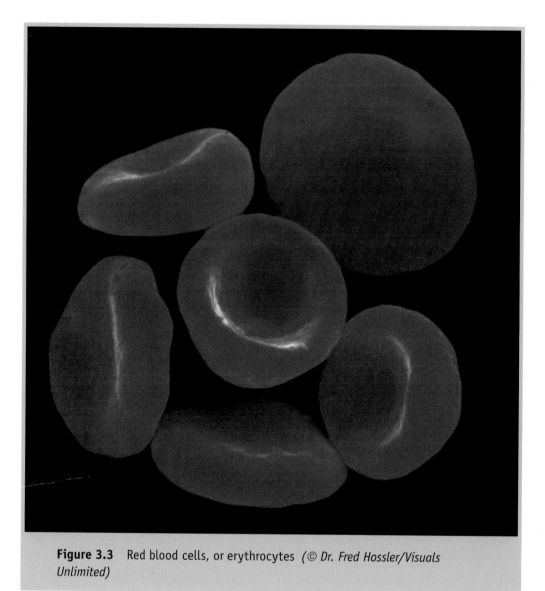

Figure 3.3   Red blood cells, or erythrocytes *(© Dr. Fred Hossler/Visuals Unlimited)*

between 5,000 and 9,000 white blood cells. Of those, between 50 and 70 percent are neutrophils, a type of leukocyte that eats invading bacteria and digests them with corrosive chemicals. Another 20 to 50 percent

Figure 3.4   Platelets are essential for blood clotting and wound healing. *(© Dr. Dennis Kunkel/Visuals Unlimited)*

are lymphocytes, specialized cells that produce **antibodies**, chemicals that recognize specifically and mark for destruction cells or bacteria that are foreign to the body. Monocytes comprise 2 to 8 percent of the leukocyte population and develop into macrophages in tissues. Macrophages are especially voracious **phagocytic** cells, meaning they will hungrily eat large numbers of invading bacteria. Another 1 to 5 percent of the leukocyte population are eosinophils, which release chemicals to damage parasites such as worms. Finally, basophils, only 0.1 percent of the population, release **histamines**, chemicals that trigger **inflammation**. Inflammation causes tissue to swell and to become red and warm, and it signals other leukocytes to come streaming to the site. Basophils are also responsible for the symptoms experienced by those who suffer from allergies.

Given the range of important functions for which blood cells are responsible, it is no surprise that interference with erythrocytes, leukocytes, or platelets produces serious physical consequences. Leukemia exerts this impact because the disease is the consequence of the overproduction of immature blood cells that do not function properly. The myeloid and lymphoid lineages have the capacity to start with nonspecialized cells and to have them become, over the course of their development, differentiated cells. With leukemia, cells get sidetracked in their development and continue to divide without ever maturing.

Depending on the specific type of leukemia, the immature cells that accumulate may not be able to carry oxygen efficiently, fight infection, or help blood to clot. By overwhelming the blood cell population, they also crowd out the normal cells that might be able to perform these tasks.

LEUKEMIC STEM CELLS

The notion that cancers might arise from "leftover," undifferentiated embryonic tissue dates back more than 150 years to the ideas of Rudolf Virchow and Julius Cohnheim, two German scientists. They based their theory on microscopic observations of tissues from fetuses and their similarities to certain types of tumors. The notion that cancer cells might be similar to embryonic cells was very appealing. After all, both cancer cells and embryonic cells underwent cell division and were unspecialized or

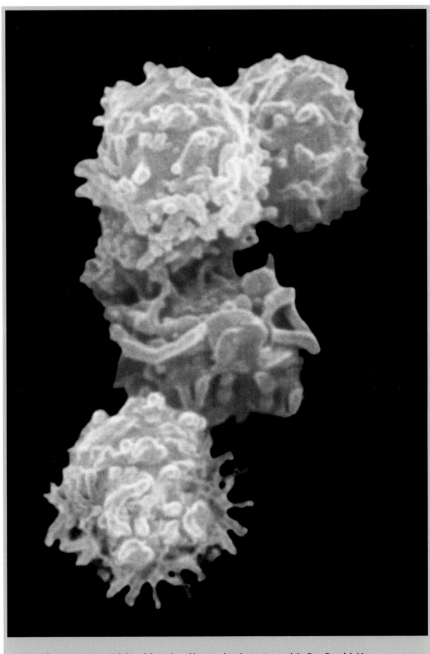

Figure 3.5   White blood cells, or leukocytes *(© Dr. David M. Phillips/Visuals Unlimited)*

undifferentiated. Also, some tissues, such as blood, keep a reserve of "embryonic-like" cells in reserve—stem cells. Like the cells seen in embryos or cancer, stem cells can keep dividing and they do not differentiate.

◆ THE LYMPHATIC SYSTEM

In addition to the circulatory system, which is composed of blood vessels and the heart, the body also has a series of lymph vessels called the lymphatic system. When blood enters a capillary, the smallest type of blood vessel, it loses fluid into the surrounding tissue. The capillary recaptures 85 percent of this fluid, and the remaining 15 percent is returned to the blood by lymph vessels.

Fluid enters the lymphatic system by diffusing into small lymph capillaries. Blood capillaries and lymph capillaries are located together. The lymph fluid is similar to the liquid found in the spaces between cells. Eventually all of the lymph re-enters the blood circulatory system via large veins located above the heart.

In addition to the vessels, the lymphatic system also contains specialized tissues. Lymph nodes are located along the lymphatic vessels; they filter the lymph and are populated by white blood cells that attack viruses, bacteria, and even cancer cells. Similarly, the spleen, tonsils, and appendix trap foreign materials and fight them with white blood cells. For this reason when a person has an infection, and in some cases cancer, lymph nodes may become tender and swollen. In addition, analyzing lymph nodes that are "downstream" from a tumor can help determine whether metastasis has occurred. Pathologists use cell staining,

In 1917 Arthur Pappenheim was the first scientist to hypothesize that normal blood cells come from a stem cell population. As we now realize, Pappenheim was correct, and it may be that aspects of Virchow and

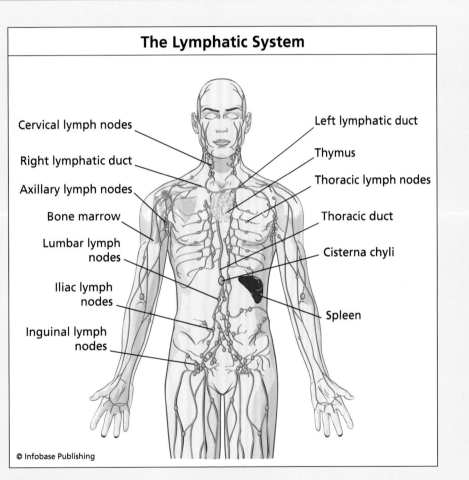

The Lymphatic System

Cervical lymph nodes

Right lymphatic duct

Axillary lymph nodes

Bone marrow

Lumbar lymph nodes

Iliac lymph nodes

Inguinal lymph nodes

Left lymphatic duct

Thymus

Thoracic lymph nodes

Thoracic duct

Cisterna chyli

Spleen

© Infobase Publishing

Figure 3.6

microscopy, and molecular techniques to detect cancer cells that have been trapped in lymph nodes.

Cohnheim's theory were as well. It is likely that all cancers derive from small populations of "cancer stem cells" and that the leukemia itself originates from a **leukemic stem cell (LSC)**.

In 1973 Ernest McCulloch isolated **myeloma** cells from a mouse. Myeloma is a type of cancer affecting lymphocytes. McCulloch examined the cells closely and found that only 1 out of 100 to 1 out of 10,000 could grow outside the mouse's body in a culture dish the way that cancer cells generally can.[2] McCulloch concluded that only a small proportion of these cancer cells behaved like stem cells, meaning they could divide and produce more cancer cells. In 1985 Jim McGriffin made similar observations in humans. McGriffin was studying human leukemia cells and demonstrated that only a small proportion of them were responsible for generating the other leukemia cells. In other words, they were behaving like stem cells.[3]

The idea that cancer cells originate from a single cell was reinforced by Philip Fialkow's demonstration that leukemic cells are **clonal** in origin. He examined the DNA of the leukemic cells and observed that it was identical, meaning the cells were the **clone** of a single original cell. Finally, in 1997 John Dick and his colleagues demonstrated the existence of a leukemic stem cell (LSC). The discovery was met with great excitement and it opened up new areas for research. Scientists are trying to understand the biology of LSC in particular and how it compares with that of normal blood stem cells, with the objective of identifying new treatments.

SUMMARY

Blood cells develop in the bone marrow, a spongy tissue found inside bones. The three major components in the blood cell population are erythrocytes, leukocytes, and platelets. Erythrocytes are important for transporting oxygen in the body; leukocytes are part of the immune system and help fight infection; and platelets are cell fragments that participate in blood clotting. All types of blood cells originate from pluripotent stem cells. There are many types of leukocytes but the broadest categories are those arising from the lymphoid lineage and those from the myeloid lineage. Leukemia cells originate from their own type of abnormal stem cell, called a leukemic stem cell (LSC).

4

LEUKEMIAS ARE NOT ALL THE SAME

KEY POINTS

- There are four major types of leukemia: acute lymphocytic leukemia (ALL), chronic lymphocytic leukemia (CLL), acute myelogenous leukemia (AML), and chronic myelogenous leukemia (CML).

- Leukemia is the most common type of cancer in children.

- ALL accounts for 75 percent of childhood leukemia cases.

- CLL is the most common type of leukemia in adults in North America and Western Europe.

- AML is generally more deadly than other types of cancer.

- CML is associated with the presence of the Philadelphia chromosome in leukemia cells.

On February 24, 1841, Peter Campbell was admitted into the Royal Infirmary in Edinburgh, Scotland. Mr. Campbell was 30 years old and a weaver by trade; he made cloth on a loom. He went to the infirmary because he felt weak and had a swollen abdomen. Mr. Campbell had started to feel ill about six weeks earlier, his principal symptom being sore joints. He had noticed the swelling in his abdomen four months previous to this visit but it had not hurt, so he had not sought medical help. Mr. Campbell reported that he had experienced "night sweats" and that he found it difficult to breathe when he exerted himself.

Although doctors were not sure what was wrong with Mr. Campbell, they kept him in the hospital, observed him, and tried to make him comfortable. By March 25, Mr. Campbell was complaining of severe pain in his head. He had a fever and his pulse was much faster than normal. On March 26, doctors bled Mr. Campbell with leeches, hoping to remove harmful substances in his blood. Unfortunately, this treatment did not help. In fact, over the next two days, Mr. Campbell worsened. Doctors bled him one more time on March 28; they removed 14 ounces of blood. Again, this treatment had no effect, and nor did anything else that doctors tried. By March 30, Mr. Campbell was very weak, fevered, and unable to eat, and his pulse was 104 beats per minute (a normal pulse ranges from 60 to 70 beats per minute). He died on April 1. His illness had killed him quickly.

Doctors autopsied Mr. Campbell's body on April 3. Two observations are particularly noteworthy. First, the abdominal swelling was due to an enlarged spleen; Mr. Campbell's weighed 7 pounds, 3.5 ounces. Recall that a normal spleen weighs less than half a pound. Second, the spleen and blood vessels throughout the body contained an abundance of white material. This material resembled pus that could have collected due to an infection, but doctors could find no evidence that an infection had been present. In fact, the abundance of the "pus" and the absence of any **abscesses** (pockets containing pus and dead cells, and that are surrounded by inflamed tissue) was strong evidence that no infection had occurred.

Looking at the description of this case with the benefit of twenty-first-century knowledge, we can readily hypothesize that Mr. Campbell suffered from leukemia. In addition to the types of information collected from examinations of him while he lived and after he died, physicians today would also collect blood to study and probably evaluate bone marrow samples to see whether leukemic cells were present, and if so the type or types of these cells. Physicians would also determine what kind of leukemia was present, because, as in the case for cancer in general, leukemia is not a single disease. Depending on the specific blood cells affected, leukemia can be divided into four major types: acute lymphocytic leukemia (ALL), **chronic lymphocytic leukemia (CLL)**,

SPOTLIGHT ON CANCER SCIENTISTS:
ERNST NEUMANN, M.D. (1834–1918)

Perhaps it is because he was a painfully quiet man or maybe it was being in a family where his son, brother, and father were famous mathematicians that prevented the Prussian scientist and physician Ernst Neumann from enjoying the place in history that he so richly deserves. Referred to as the "father of hematology," Neumann discovered that blood cells are produced in bone marrow.

Neumann was born in 1834 and earned his degree from the University of Königsberg in 1850. He also earned his M.D. in 1855 and then continued his training in labs in Prague, Berlin, and then back in Königsberg. In Berlin, Neumann studied under the guidance of Rudolf Virchow. In 1859 Neumann was appointed a lecturer in medicine, and in 1866 he was

acute myelogenous leukemia (AML), and **chronic myelogenous leukemia (CML)**. Acute and chronic refer to the rate at which the disease advances; acute is rapid and chronic is slow. Lymphocytic and myelogenous indicate whether the leukemia cells originated with the lymphoid or myeloid lineages, respectively. The symptoms of all types of leukemia share similarities such as fatigue, increased infections, and easier bruising. Diagnostic procedures are also alike for all leukemia types; doctors collect blood and bone marrow to determine what specific type of leukemia cells is present. What does differ quite a bit among the various leukemias is typical age of onset, **prognosis** or predictions about the course of the disease, and treatment.

---

promoted to Professor of Pathology. He remained in Königsberg for the rest of his life.

In 1868 Neumann described his observations of the bone marrows of humans and rabbits. He had squeezed the marrow out of the bones and observed it microscopically. He discovered that the marrow contained red blood cells that had nuclei. In contrast, mature red blood cells in mammals do not have nuclei. Consequently, Neumann concluded that red blood cells are made and develop in the marrow. Subsequent to this discovery, he revealed that white blood cells are also produced in the marrow. Moreover, Neumann postulated that a single type of renewable stem cell gave rise to all of the cells of the blood. This idea was ahead of its time and was not accepted by his contemporaries.

Neumann continued his research throughout his life, making several other discoveries including that of myelogenous leukemia. He died in 1918.

ACUTE LYMPHOCYTIC LEUKEMIA (ALL)

Acute leukemias are generally rare, accounting for approximately 2 percent of all cancers in the United States. Leukemia is, however, the most common type of cancer in children and ALL accounts for 75 percent of childhood leukemia. This disease occurs more commonly in children and young adults than in older people. Diagnosis of ALL generally occurs between the of ages 2 and 8; the peak incidence is at 4 years. Each year approximately 4,000 new cases of ALL are diagnosed in the United States. In 2006, of 22,280 people who died of leukemia, 1,490 had suffered with ALL.[1] The diagnosis of ALL depends on physical examination of the patient as well as close examination of the blood and bone marrow. If ALL is suspected, **immunophenotyping** is also done. This technique allows physicians to determine exactly what kind of lymphocyte is abnormal. Knowing the precise nature of the ALL is important for providing effective treatment.

The causes of ALL are not well understood. Exposure to high doses of **radiation** increases risk, as does living in a developed country or being socioeconomically advantaged. ALL is one of the few cancers that occurs in lower numbers in poor people.

Treatment of children with ALL has been very successful; survival rates are as high as 90 percent. Unfortunately, adults with ALL fare less well than children. Adult survival ranges from 40 to 65 percent.[2]

CHRONIC LYMPHOCYTIC LEUKEMIA (CLL)

CLL is the most common form of leukemia in adults in Western countries. More than 10,000 people are diagnosed each year in the United States alone. CLL is quite uncommon in individuals before the age of 45. In fact, more than 95 percent of CLL patients are more than 50 years

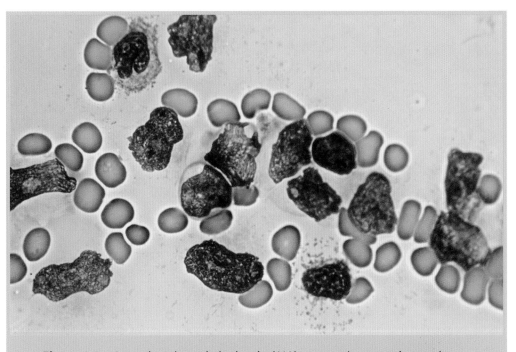

Figure 4.1 Acute lymphocytic leukemia (ALL) causes the excessive production of immature white blood cells (purple). This excess of immature white blood cells limits the space in the bone marrow for normal red blood cells, white blood cells, and platelets. The resulting lowered levels of these normal cells causes the various symptoms of the disease. *(© Biology Media/Photo Researchers, Inc.)*

old. Because CLL comes on slowly and gradually, symptoms can easily go unnoticed. Most CLL patients are diagnosed after a routine checkup. The physician notices an enlarged lymph node and enlarged spleen and consequently orders a blood test to see if the blood cells are normal. If this test reveals an overabundance of leukocytes, the doctor will order additional tests to examine the bone marrow to determine exactly what type of lymphocyte is involved, and also to have cells analyzed to see whether chromosomes are damaged in any way.

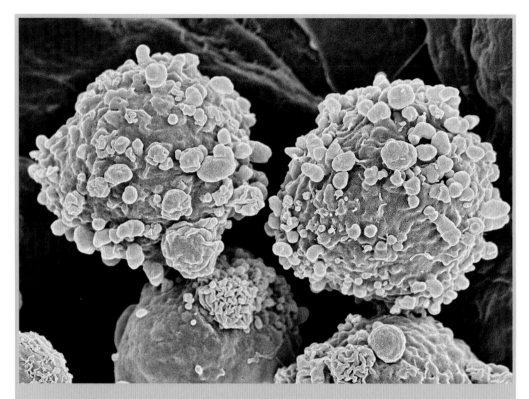

Figure 4.2 This colored scanning electron micrograph (SEM) shows white blood cells from a patient with chronic lymphocytic leukemia (CLL); this form of leukemia causes the excessive production of lymphocytes. This form of leukemia is most often found in the elderly. *(© Steve Gschmeissner/Photo Researchers, Inc.)*

Scientists have not determined the causes of CLL, but they have have identified several risk factors. For example, CLL is more common in males and in white people of European ancestry than in individuals of Asian ancestry. A comparison of CLL incidence in China and the United States underscores the role of ethnicity. In China, CLL accounted for only 4 to 6 percent of all leukemias among hospitalized patients in Beijing, whereas 30 percent of adult leukemia in the United States is CLL.[3,4] Furthermore, studies of migrating human populations show that ethnic groups retain their risk for CLL associated with their geographical origin rather than assuming the risk associated with their new location. Put another way, a white adult from the United States who moves to Beijing will not enjoy the same lower risk for CLL that Chinese people do. Additional studies that examined the family patterns of CLL incidence suggest that there is a hereditary factor that affects the susceptibility to developing CLL. Alone, this factor will not cause CLL, but if a person has it and is exposed to additional risk factors, the likelihood of developing CLL increases. CLL shows the highest family incidence of any of the major blood cancers.

Other risk factors include exposure to pesticides or the chemicals used in farming. For example, one class of herbicides, phenoxy, is associated with an increased CLL risk. More specifically, the herbicides 2, 4, 5-T and 2, 4-D are candidates for increasing the risk of CLL. Although 2, 4, 5-T use has been restricted by law, herbicides containing 2, 4-D are readily available for sale not only to farmers but also to shoppers at the local gardening store.

Because CLL generally advances slowly, most physicians will take a "watchful-waiting" approach to treatment. The initial bone marrow sample and biopsy serves as a baseline against which other samples can be compared to make sure the disease is not out of control. In many cases of CLL, it is better for the patient to "maintain" the disease rather than undergo radiation or chemotherapy treatments that might diminish the quality of life without eliminating the cancer. If treatment becomes necessary, physicians will take action.

Also, that initial bone marrow biopsy will come in handy as a baseline to check whether treatments are working. The survival rate for CLL is approximately 75 percent. Of 22,280 people who died of leukemia in 2006, CLL was the culprit in 600 cases.[5]

ACUTE MYELOGENOUS LEUKEMIA (AML)

Unlike ALL and CLL, AML is the result of stem cells in the myeloid lineage becoming cancer cells. Approximately 12,000 new cases are diagnosed per year in the United States. Compared to other types of leukemia, AML is the most deadly. Of 22,280 people who died of leukemia in 2006, 9,040 were AML cases. The age of onset is generally later in life, but AML accounts for 15 to 20 percent of childhood leukemia. The risk of AML increases with age. Among 30- to 34-year-olds, AML incidence is 1 in 100,000 people. In contrast, incidence increases to 1 in 10,000 people in people between the ages of 65 to 69. The **median** age of diagnosis is 65 years. The likelihood of death due to AML is also related to age. The overall survival rate is only 20 percent, but it reaches greater than 50 percent for AML patients under the age of 15 years.[6]

AML occurs when there is disruption in the function of a **transcription factor**, a molecule that binds to DNA and regulates gene expression. The cells affected by this faulty transcription factor are stem cells in either the **granulocyte** or monocyte lineage. Granulocytes are a type of white blood cell that contain little packets of enzymes to destroy microorganisms, whereas monocytes are a type of white blood cell that develops into macrophages. Macrophages are phagocytic cells, meaning that they eat debris and invading microorganisms that enter the body. There are eight different subtypes of AML, and identifying the type is essential for predicting the course of the disease and treating the patient effectively.

One type of treatment that has shown hopeful signs of success is differentiation therapy. The idea behind the approach is that if cancer cells could be forced to mature and differentiate, the malignant state could be shifted to a benign one wherein cells would no longer divide without control. The goal of differentiation therapy is to regulate genes in

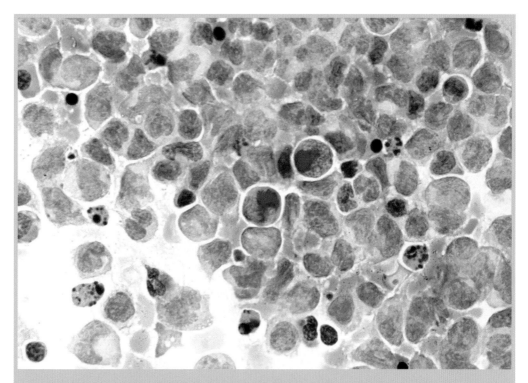

Figure 4.3   Acute myelocytic leukemia (AML) causes the formation of an abnormally large number of myelocyte white blood cells. (Dr. Lance Liotta Laboratory/National Cancer Institute/U.S. National Institutes of Health)

cancer cells so that growth can be halted and, if necessary, **apoptosis**, or programmed cell death, can be triggered.

Differentiation therapy has produced very promising results with **acute promyelocytic leukemia (APL)**, a subtype of AML. Patients treated with all-trans retinoic acid (ATRA), a retinoid, which is a type of signaling molecule found in embryos, go into remission immediately; cancer cells stop dividing. Treatment of APL with ATRA has achieved 80 percent survival after five years. Prior to this type of therapy, APL was very deadly.

As is the case with ALL and CLL, the cause of AML is not understood; however, scientists have been able to identify risk factors. Exposure to high doses of radiation, benzene, or even therapeutic radiation, depending upon dose and duration, increases the likelihood of developing AML. Tobacco smoke and chemicals that alter DNA or inhibit the repair of damaged DNA also increase risk. Sadly, chemotherapy for breast cancer, ovarian cancer, or lymphoma can also make a patient more vulnerable to developing AML. Such "collateral damage" resulting in the development of a **secondary cancer** is one of the potential, unfortunate side effects of treatments aimed at destroying a primary cancer.

CHRONIC MYELOGENOUS LEUKEMIA (CML)

CML accounts for 15 to 20 percent of all leukemias. This type of leukemia, which generally occurs only in adults, represents less than 3 percent of leukemia in individuals between infancy and 19 years. It is very rare in children; fewer than 50 cases per year are diagnosed in the United States. Among all age groups, approximately 4,000 cases are diagnosed per year in the United States. The median age of diagnosis is approximately 50 years. Although the overall survival for CML is a little more than 40 percent, the disease progresses very slowly in many cases. Of 22,280 people who died of leukemia in 2006, only 600 died from CML.[7]

CML has been particularly well studied. The specific defect in the stem cell that causes leukemia has been discovered; as a consequence, effective drugs have been developed that produce very high rates of remission, provided the treatment is started early enough in the disease.

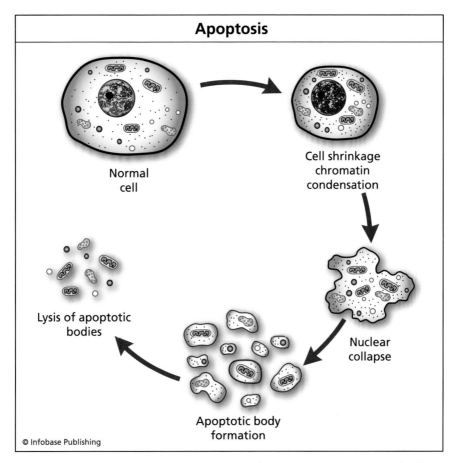

Apoptosis

Normal
cell

Cell shrinkage
chromatin
condensation

Nuclear
collapse

Apoptotic body
formation

Lysis of apoptotic
bodies

© Infobase Publishing

Figure 4.4 This diagram shows the stages of apoptosis, or programmed cell death.

CML has three disease phases. The **chronic phase** comes first. It can last anywhere from months to years with 3 to 5 years being common. Few, if any, symptoms are evident. A person could be in the chronic phase and have no idea that he or she was sick. Next comes the **accelerated phase**, which can last 3 to 9 months. During this interval, cells are accumulating more genetic errors and increasing the production of abnormal cells. Finally, the **blast crisis** can last from 3 to 6 months.

◆ DRUG DEVELOPMENT

The path starting with the research and development of new drugs to testing in humans and making these new medicines available to all patients is a long, painstaking, and careful one. The FDA is responsible for monitoring and approving each step of the process.

First, preclinical research includes the development, synthesis, and purification of the drug itself and then an evaluation of its safety in at least two species of laboratory animals. Next, clinical studies attempt to determine whether the drug is safe, is effective, and does not produce side effects that outweigh its benefits. Clinical studies are done in stages. In Phase 1, patients and/or healthy volunteers are given the test drug. They are monitored for the body's response to the drug as well as the side effects that might occur with increasing doses. Phase 2 of the clinical studies is done with patients who have the disease or condition to see if treatment is effective. Phase 3 expands the drug testing to larger human populations. In all phases of testing from preclinical to clinical, the studies are carefully controlled and subjects are carefully monitored. Every step of the process and its results are also submitted to the FDA for review. If all goes well, the drug is approved for marketing in the United States. Although there is variability in how long it takes from the development of a drug through testing and appearance on the market, the average time is 8.5 years.

During this time, the leukemia cells accumulate even more genetic errors, especially in tumor suppressor genes. The cells proliferate very rapidly and are resistant to signals telling them to undergo apoptosis and die. If untreated, the blast crisis is fatal.

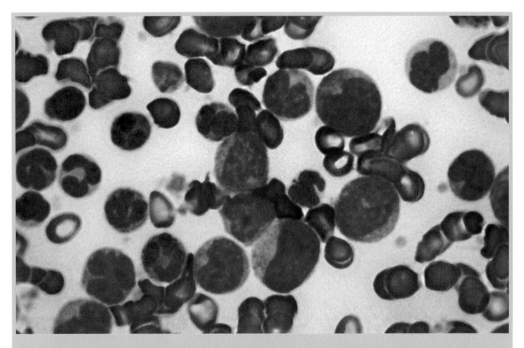

Figure 4.5 This blood smear shows the blast crisis phase of chronic myelogenous leukemia (CML). *(Stacy Howard/Centers for Disease Control and Prevention/ U.S. Department of Health and Human Services)*

The defect observed in 95 percent of CML patients is a structure called the Philadelphia chromosome. Discovered in 1960 by the U.S. scientists Peter Nowell and David Hungerford, this abnormal chromosome is the consequence of chromosome breakage and abnormal rejoining in a stem cell of the myeloid lineage. Specifically, a piece of chromosome 9 breaks off and joins to the broken end of chromosome 22. The Philadelphia chromosome, derived from chromosome 22, is then visibly shortened. Because the event occurs in a stem cell, all cells derived from it also possess these altered chromosomes.

The rearrangement of genes caused by this chromosome breakage and rejoining causes cancer because gene function has been altered.

Chromosome 9 possesses a gene called *abl* that encodes for **tyrosine kinase**, a type of protein involved in the communication pathway that regulated cell division. When *abl* is attached to a site called *bcr* on chromosome 22, the resulting fused *bcr/abl* gene encodes for an abnormal tyrosine kinase. This dysfunctional tyrosine kinase does not communicate properly with the other molecules that turn it on and off. In fact, this bcr/abl tyrosine kinase is stuck "on." No matter what signals the cell receives, it undergoes cell division. Cells with tyrosine

---

◆ THE SEED AND SOIL HYPOTHESIS

Once a tumor metastasizes to other parts of the body, cancer becomes more difficult to treat and the prognosis may be more dire. When cancer cells break away from a tumor and enter the circulatory system, they tend to make secondary tumors in predictable locations. For example, melanoma, a type of malignant skin cancer, spreads to lungs; and colon cancer cells take up residence in the liver. In the case of leukemia, common metastasis destinations include the brain, spine, and heart. The existence of relationships between the sites of primary tumors and the secondary tumors that originate from them suggests that some organs and tissues are more "welcoming" to metastatic cells. Why might this be so?

In 1889, the British physician Stephen Paget published a paper in which he described case histories of cancer patients that led him to propose the "seed and soil hypothesis." According to this idea, cancer cells are carried in all directions when metastasis occurs, but they can only grow in tissues that are "congenial." In other words, the metastatic cells would grow only in organs somehow predisposed to forming secondary tumors. Paget's ideas

kinase permanently "on" do not stop dividing. The cells have become cancerous.

The cause of the chromosome breakage that creates the Philadelphia chromosome is not known. It is clear that exposure to high doses of radiation, but not to dental or medical X-rays, increases the risk of CML. Other risk factors have not been identified but undoubtedly exist because not everyone who develops CML has been exposed to intense radiation.

were at odds with his professional contemporaries who thought that cancer cells spread through the lymph and simply lodged in tissues distant from the original tumor. Scientists proposed that the metastatic cells redirected the new surrounding tissue to become cancerous itself.

Paget had evidence on his side. He thought that if metastatic cancer cells could form tumors wherever they lodged, then secondary tumors should be located randomly. They are not. Paget analyzed 735 case histories and showed that breast cancers spread to the liver more often than to any other organ. Despite being correct, Paget's hypothesis was not appreciated in his time.

The seed and soil hypothesis was resurrected in 1980 by the U.S. scientists Ian Hart and Isaiah Fidler. Using clinical information about the susceptibility of certain organs to metastasis as well as techniques to track individual cells to their destinations, and observing whether or not secondary tumors form, Hart and Fidler added more evidence that supports Paget's hypothesis. In fact, researchers are hard at work trying to learn what it is in a tissue that supports the growth of metastatic cancer cells and why certain primary tumor cells get preference for this growth.

Because scientists know the molecular genetic and biochemical defect that leads to CML, efforts to design effective drugs have been very successful. The chemotherapy drug Gleevec (imatinib) inhibits the abnormal kinase that is made by CML cells. Imatinib treatment is most effective when it is initiated early on in the course of the disease. Under optimal conditions, imatinib can produce a 96 percent remission rate. Eventually, imatinib can lose its effectiveness as leukemic cells acquire resistance. Although there are drugs that can be used as a second line of defense drugs, the only way to actually *cure* CML is to do a bone marrow transplant. This procedure removes the abnormal stem cells and replaces them with normal ones, which then produce normal blood cells.

SUMMARY

Leukemia is not a single disease. In fact, there are four major types: acute lymphocytic leukemia (ALL), chronic lymphocytic leukemia (CLL), acute myelogenous leukemia (AML), and chronic myelogenous leukemia (CML). These leukemias differ in the age of onset, causes and risk factors, treatment, and the likelihood of survival.

5

CHILDHOOD LEUKEMIA

KEY POINTS

- Leukemia accounts for approximately 25 percent of all childhood cancers.

- Leukemia in children is almost always acute, not chronic.

- Infant leukemia is a subset of childhood leukemia.

- The symptoms of childhood cancer are similar to those seen in adults.

- The cause(s) of childhood leukemia are not known. Two hypotheses are exposure to pesticides, and high energy radiation.

- Tremendous progress has been made in treating childhood leukemia successfully.

- Some of the treatments can produce long-term side effects including secondary cancers.

Jennifer Stroud was a normal, happy 5-year-old girl who lived in Dallas, Texas, with her mother, father, brother, and favorite doll Molly. On Thanksgiving Day 1993, Jennifer's family noticed that she was tiring easily and running a low-grade fever. She also had more than the "usual" number of bruises expected on a 5-year-old. Her parents were not immediately worried but when Jennifer did not improve and her parents realized that she was bruising very easily, they decided to have her examined by their doctor.

Jennifer's doctor ran some blood tests and on December 24, 1993, Jennifer was admitted into the hospital because the preliminary tests suggested that she had leukemia. Additional tests confirmed this diagnosis; the evening of that same day, Jennifer's parents learned that their daughter had AML. Physicians initiated emergency treatment. They did a procedure called **leukapheresis***, which filters the blood to reduce the number of abnormal leukocytes. Jennifer's condition was critical.*

Jennifer began chemotherapy right away. Three rounds of treatment were planned, and Jennifer's family and medical caregivers were delighted when she went into remission after only two rounds. Unfortunately, Jennifer had to endure some terrible side effects brought on by her chemotherapy. She lost her hair and her appetite. She had a sore throat, developed skin rashes, and bruised even more easily and deeply. Even worse, Jennifer's eyes dehydrated so much that she could not see and she had fevers spike to 106°F. Physicians prescribed other drugs to help reduce these side effects and Jennifer recovered enough to come home. Sadly, her leukemia came roaring back by April 29, 1994.

Jennifer's parents had some difficult choices to make. They wanted their daughter to survive but did not wish for her to suffer any more. They decided to forego another round of chemotherapy and instead opted to have physicians try a bone marrow transplant. Jennifer's parents also turned their energies toward identifying nutritional and other types of treatments to lessen side effects and improve their daughter's quality of life.

Bone marrow transplantation requires a close biochemical match between the cells of the donor and those of the person receiving the transplant. If the molecules on the cell membranes of the donor and recipient are very different, the recipient's body will "reject" the transplant. The transplanted cells will not survive. The usual procedure for identifying a good donor is to test close relatives. Unfortunately for Jennifer, neither of her parents nor any close relative was a suitable match. The Strouds tried the next option; they searched for a donor through the National Marrow Donor Program. This effort was more successful—they identified a donor in Canada.

Jennifer's bone marrow transplant was performed in September 1994. She returned home in October 1994, but had to be isolated from people until she had enough healthy leukocytes in her body to fight off infections. Jennifer was physically weak but her parents did everything they could to strengthen her through nutrition and other remedies. As Jennifer's energy and stamina improved, she was sometimes able to attend school and play with her friends. She also wrote to other sick children to encourage and help them.

As hard as Jennifer and her family fought, this battle was not going to be won. On February 2, 1995, Jennifer's leukemia was back. The bone marrow transplant did not cure her. The physicians told Jennifer's parents that she would survive no longer than another month, and that the only remaining option was to try an experimental drug. Unwilling to let any possibility go untried, they agreed and combined this new chemotherapy with specific nutritional approaches. Jennifer's condition was stable throughout almost all of 1995 but her leukemia returned once more. Nothing more could be done; Jennifer died February 1, 1996. She was eight years old.[1,2]

TYPES OF LEUKEMIA IN CHILDREN

Leukemia is the most common type of cancer occurring in children. It accounts for approximately 25 percent of all childhood cancers. Approximately 2,200 children are affected each year in the United States alone. Leukemias in children are almost always acute, not chronic. Roughly 60 to 75 percent of leukemias are ALL, 25 to 38 percent are AML, and 2 to 5 percent are CML. CML is very rare in children; fewer than 50 cases are diagnosed each year in the United States. Interestingly, most leukemias in children originate from the lymphoid lineage, whereas in adults 85 percent of leukemias are myeloid.[3,4,5]

Infant leukemia, which is diagnosed within the first 12 months of life, is another subset of childhood leukemia. The biology of the disease in infants is different from what is seen with older children. For example, leukemia appearing in infancy is slightly more predominant in females, whereas in older children it is more likely to occur in males. Also, leukocyte counts are already very high and leukemia has often spread to the brain and spinal cord by the time of diagnosis in infant leukemia. It appears likely that most, if not all, cases of infant leukemia arise *in utero*, before a baby is born. Scientists hypothesize that infant leukemia originates from a stem cell that did not fully commit to normal development and differentiation.

Children with leukemia experience the same range of symptoms as those seen in adults. They tire easily, bruise and bleed more, get frequent nosebleeds, and are susceptible to infection. Leukemic children also lose their appetites and may experience bone pain and nausea. In 12 percent of children with AML, and 6 percent with ALL, leukemic cells metastasize or spread to the brain and spinal cord. This metastasis can result in severe headaches, seizures, problems with balance, and altered vision. Sometimes ALL can spread to the lymph nodes inside the

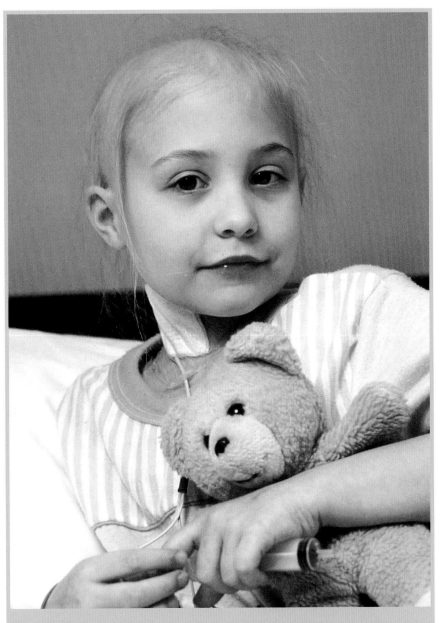

Figure 5.1   This young girl is receiving chemotherapy for acute lymphocytic leukemia (ALL). The majority of childhood leukemias are ALL. *(Bill Branson/National Cancer Institute/U.S. National Institutes of Health)*

chest. When this event occurs, the **trachea**, or windpipe, can become "crowded" so breathing becomes impaired. This metastasis to the chest lymph nodes can also interfere with blood vessels, thus impeding the flow of blood to and from the heart.

LEUKEMIA IN TWINS

The first published description of identical twins who both developed leukemia was in 1882. Since then approximately 70 cases have been reported. If one identical twin develops leukemia before 6 years of age, the other twin has a 20 to 25 percent chance of developing ALL or AML. In contrast, siblings of childhood leukemia patients, even nonidentical twins, have only twice the low level of risk faced by all children.[6] More specifically, children face less than a 1 percent chance of developing leukemia by age 20, and the siblings of leukemic children have less than a 2 percent incidence of developing the disease by the end of their teens. Leukemia in identical twins apparently starts *in utero*. A stem cell becomes leukemic in one twin, and then when it undergoes repeated cell divisions, some of the newly produced cancer cells spread to the other twin through the **placenta**, which connects both of their circulatory systems. Scientists have shown that identical twins share a single bloodstream and placenta, the structure in the mother that delivers oxygen and food molecules through a network of blood vessels.

DIAGNOSIS OF CHILDHOOD LEUKEMIA

Determining whether a child has leukemia uses similar methods to those needed to diagnose an adult. Generally parents first notice that their child is tiring more easily and seems "not right." A trip to the pediatrician and a physical exam might reveal swollen lymph nodes and/or a swollen spleen, evident by feeling the left side of the abdomen. The physician would run blood tests to see what kinds of cells are present, whether they are there in adequate numbers, and if any abnormal cells are observed. If appropriate, the doctor would next take a sample of bone marrow and a pathologist, a medical scientist who studies disease, would evaluate whether abnormal stem cells and leukemic cells were present. Similarly, the child's lymph nodes would also be **biopsied**, or examined for the presence of cancer cells. Finally, a child suspected of having leukemia might also undergo a **lumbar puncture**, a procedure by which a doctor inserts a needle into the spinal column, and collects spinal fluid. The pathologist examines the spinal fluid to see whether any cancer cells are present.

WHAT CAUSES CHILDHOOD LEUKEMIA?

As is true for all forms of leukemia, scientists are not exactly sure about what causes the disease. In the case of childhood leukemia, research interest is intense. The vision of babies and young children suffering from leukemia, or any cancer for that matter, is so powerful that fund-raising for leukemia research has been very successful. Similarly, the National Institutes of Health (NIH), a resource funded by the United States government, provides competitive grants for scientists studying leukemia and other diseases. Leukemia in children packs an understandably emotional punch, and there are many families, physicians, and scientists who have devoted their lives to figuring out causes, treatments, and prevention. These efforts are bearing fruit because scientists have learned more about risk factors associated with childhood leukemia than they know about adult forms of the disease.

Childhood leukemia cannot be attributed to one specific risk factor. As with most cancers, the potential causes are cumulative and people vary in their susceptibilities. It is likely that any individual children who develop leukemia do so because of their own particular exposures to risk, their innate susceptibility probably due in part to their genes, and chance. Information about risk factors is, however, valuable because it can help with prevention.

Many scientists hypothesize that childhood leukemia may be related to the inadequate development of an infant's immune system. Alternatively, the disease may originate because an infant was not exposed to the common infections that occur in early childhood. In both cases, exposure to common infections later might trigger a dysfunctional immune response, including the abnormal proliferation of poorly developed leukocytes.

Some observations support this hypothesis. For example, studies have revealed that children who have had ear infections in early childhood have a reduced risk of leukemia. Similarly, other studies have shown that the absence of exposure to common infections, not just ear infections, during the first year of life increases the risk for leukemias, and ALL specifically. Interestingly, childhood leukemia is more prevalent in socioeconomically advanced, developed countries, than in poor, developing nations. For example, the incidence of ALL in children between the ages of 2 and 5 years is 10 times higher in the United States, United Kingdom, and Japan than it is in Africa. Scientists think this relationship strengthens the hypothesis about the association between exposure to infection during the first year of life and the development of leukemia. Their idea is that children in affluent, developed countries are generally more isolated from crowds of people and from "dirt" than are children in developing countries.[7,8,9,10] In fact, some scientists suggest that affluent parents are overly concerned with hygiene and keep their children "too clean." Obviously they are not arguing that babies or young children should be neglected, but they wonder whether well-intentioned parents have gone too far in protecting their offspring from exposure to the natural messiness of ordinary life.

Another tantalizing idea about childhood leukemia is that there are cases that are actually caused by an infection in susceptible individuals. Although no specific virus or bacterium has been identified, there have been observations of disease patterns that support this notion. One example of such a pattern occurred in Fallon, Nevada. This town experienced an unusually high incidence of childhood leukemia. Between 1997 and 2002, there were 16 cases in all: Three of these children died, and 15 out of the 16 cases were ALL. The entire population of Fallon was only around 7,500. Scientists who studied the incidence of leukemia in this population concluded that this number of cases occurring randomly and without direct cause was an event of such low probability that one would expect to see it once every 22,000 years. Although scientists tried to identify possible causes including exposure to chemical pollution, they ultimately hypothesized that the Fallon "cancer cluster" resulted from a local epidemic that was triggered by the mixing of a large population into their relatively small rural one. Experts suggest that the origin of this particular epidemic was the arrival of 100,000 people from outside the area, who entered the town for nearby military operations. Scientists speculate that this large "foreign" population brought with it new microbes to which the children of Fallon had never been exposed.[11] As happened when Europeans first came to North America, a previously isolated population exposed to a new microbe resulted in illness among susceptible individuals.

Given that childhood leukemia can develop so early, initiating even before birth, scientists realized that it made sense to examine the effects of maternal exposure to risk factors and the development

◆ CURCUMIN: WONDER DRUG?

In addition to the development of new drugs to fight diseases like leukemia, scientists are also looking to ancient remedies and nutrition in the search for additional treatments. The spice turmeric has been used for thousands of years in Ayurvedic medicine from India. Turmeric is also a common ingredient in Asian cooking. Interestingly, the incidence of childhood leukemia is lower in Asia compared to other places in the world. Is there a relationship between turmeric and cancer prevention?

Scientists have focused their attentions on curcumin, the compound in turmeric that gives it a vivid yellow color. Experiments have shown that curcumin can prevent human leukemia cells from multiplying in culture. Other experiments revealed that curcumin was able to induce apoptosis, or cell death, in two different types of leukemia cells in culture. More experiments in mice demonstrated that curcumin restored the population of immune cells that fight cancer cells. And yet more experimentation has shown that curcumin slows metastasis, slows the process called **angiogenesis** in which blood vessels grow to connect tumors to the circulatory system, triggers apoptosis in several types of cancer cells, and stops inflammation. The preclinical findings have been so positive that human trials are under way to see whether curcumin can be developed as an effective weapon in the arsenal to fight cancer.

of leukemia in children. Maternal diet was influential. Studies showed that pregnant women who supplemented their diets with folate decreased the risk of leukemia in their children. Similarly, experiments with rodents demonstrated that a diet in which calories were somewhat restricted, and that contained both the spice curcumin and the oil geraniol, protected against the development of leukemia induced by radiation or chemical exposure. In contrast, pregnant women who ingested high amounts of bioflavinoids such as fruits and vegetables that contain quercetin, soybeans, tea, cocoa, wine, and caffeine, increased the risk of infant leukemia, particularly AML.[12] This finding should not be overinterpreted. A healthy, balanced diet during pregnancy is essential, and fruits and vegetables are a critical component. It is important to eat a varied, balanced diet and not focus on any single food.

Why would maternal folate consumption decrease leukemia risk whereas eating too many bioflavinoid-containing foods increase it? The answer resides in understanding what each of these types of molecules does to DNA. All cancers, including leukemia, are fundamentally genetic diseases in that they develop from damaged or mutated genes that lose the capacity to regulate cell division. Therefore any chemical that causes DNA damage or permits it to go uncorrected will increase the risk of cancer. In contrast, any chemical that prevents DNA damage or helps with repair will decrease the risk of cancer. In the specific case of leukemia, bioflavinoids increase risk because they can cause a break in DNA molecules and inhibit an enzyme, **topoisomerese II**, which is essential for DNA repair. Folate, on the other hand, helps prevent DNA breaks and the consequent damage.

Exposure of children to several physical and chemical factors also increase leukemia incidence. In many cases, exposure to these factors *in utero* increases the risk of leukemia even more. Examples of possible risk factors include exposure to high doses of radiation, including treatment for other types of cancer; chemotherapy for other cancers;

SPOTLIGHT ON CANCER SCIENTISTS:
SIDNEY A. FARBER, M.D. (1903–1973)

When Sidney Farber, an American physician, was working as a pathologist in Boston, Massachusetts, at Children's Hospital in the mid-1940s, the prognosis for patients with leukemia was grim. In fact, it had not really changed appreciably since the 1840s when leukemia was first described. Farber was intensely driven to cure cancer. He reasoned that science could succeed in this endeavor with creative and energetic research, adequate resources, and the will to persist.

Born in 1903 in Buffalo, New York, the third of 14 children, Farber earned his M.D. from Harvard Medical School in 1927. His clinical experiences working with young patients at Children's Hospital may have provided the spark that caused him to devote his life to curing childhood cancer. In the mid-1940s, Farber considered research that had been conducted during World War II to treat **pernicious anemia** and **tropical anemia**. Both of these diseases involve the production of an excess of immature blood cells that crowd the bone marrow. Scientists discovered that treatment with vitamin B12 could cure pernicious anemia and that folic acid was successful against tropical anemia. Because leukemia is also a problem with bone marrow function, Farber thought a similar treatment might work with leukemia. He knew that folic acid stimulates bone marrow growth and wondered what would happen if he blocked the normal action of folic acid found in the body. Could a treatment be developed that would stop the production of abnormal bone marrow in leukemic patients?

In late 1947, Farber tested aminopterin, a molecule with a structure similar to folic acid, on 16 children with ALL. To his delight, 10 of the children had temporary remissions. Since this first demonstration of remission of any leukemia, many other scientists have advanced chemotherapeutic treatments not only for ALL, but for other leukemias as well.

Farber made additional research breakthroughs in the 1950s and 1960s, most notably the discovery that treatment with actinomycin D and radiation would pro-

Figure 5.2 Dr. Sidney Farber. *(National Library of Medicine/U.S. National Institutes of Health)*

duce remission in **Wilms' tumor**, a type of kidney cancer that occurs in children. Starting in the 1950s and continuing until his death in 1973, Farber acted as a "medical diplomat," regularly presenting information at congressional hearings to increase federal support for cancer research. He was successful in this task: The annual budget of the National Cancer Institute, only $48 million in 1957, had more than tripled to $167 million by 1967.[13]

immunosuppressive drugs taken after organ transplantation; certain other diseases such as **Down syndrome**, **Li-Fraumeni syndrome**, and **Fanconi's anemia** to mention three examples; and exposure to pesticides.

The association between pesticides and childhood leukemia has been especially well studied, probably because this risk factor could be eliminated. Scientists have demonstrated that exposure to pesticides indoors is more dangerous than outdoors. In particular, the use of pest strips indoors is strongly associated with leukemia. Scientists have also determined that children are more likely to develop leukemia after pesticide exposure if they are very young, and fetuses are at increased risk *in utero.* Exposure to pesticides from professional extermination is most dangerous during the ages of 12 to 24 months. Scientists have also examined other potential risks that so far have not yielded any clear association with childhood leukemia. For example, studies of the unfortunate nuclear reactor accident at Chernobyl have not revealed any relationship between exposure to low levels of radiation and development of infant leukemia. Similarly, no studies have found evidence for an association between proximity to electrical installations or to magnetic fields and leukemia incidence.

TREATMENT

The vigorous research effort on childhood leukemia has also yielded wonderfully effective treatments. Whereas nearly 100 percent of children with leukemia died in 1950, by 2000, only 25 percent did so. Today, remission rates exceed 90 percent and the majority of children remain permanently in this state.

The specific treatment plan designed by physicians depends upon the specific type of leukemia and how serious the disease is at the time of diagnosis. For example, with ALL, there are three phases of treatment. The first, induction therapy, is designed to kill the leukemia cells in the blood and bone marrow. The goal of this first phase is to induce remission. The second phase is called consolidation or intensification therapy. The objective here is to kill any remaining leukemia cells that are not dividing but might do so in the future. Consolidation therapy is done to prevent a relapse or recurrence of leukemia. The third phase is maintenance therapy, in which lower doses of treatments are given to kill any remaining leukemia cells. The specific tools or methods used for treatment are chemotherapy, **radiation therapy**, and stem cell transplantation. Chemotherapy refers to the administration of drugs designed to kill cancer cells. With radiation therapy, high-energy X-rays are used to kill cancer cells. Stem cell transplantations are done when it is necessary to replace the normal stem cells if they are destroyed by chemotherapy or radiation. In most cases these treatments would be used in combination.

Many cancer treatments produce undesirable side effects. For example, short-term side effects of chemotherapy include hair loss, nausea, and vomiting. Radiation therapy makes a patient extremely fatigued after treatments. There can also be long-term health consequences due to treatment. For instance, curing ALL in children can negatively impact their physical and intellectual development. In fact, treatment for ALL inhibits production of growth hormone. As a consequence, ALL survivors are much shorter than 95 percent of children their age. Fortunately, recent studies have shown that childhood survivors of ALL can be treated safely with growth hormones in order to regain height.

The most serious potential side effect from the treatment of childhood leukemia is the development of secondary cancers. Because ALL is one of the most curable forms of childhood cancer, there is a population of survivors who have lived for decades after treatment. The risk to ALL survivors for secondary cancers far exceeds the cancer risk of the general population. Scientists studied the incidence of secondary cancers in 2,169 children and adolescents who had been treated for ALL between 1962 and 1998. Of the 1,290 patients who remained in complete remission, 95 percent developed a secondary cancer.[14] The most common forms of these cancers were **meningioma**, a tumor near the brain and spinal cord, and **basal cell carcinoma**, a tumor of epithelial tissue. Other types of cancers that developed included myeloma, a type of bone marrow cancer; **lymphoma**, which affects the lymph nodes; brain tumors; carcinoma, an epithelial cell cancer; and **sarcoma**, a tumor of connective tissue.

The treatment of childhood leukemia is one of the greatest medical success stories of the twentieth century. The majority of children have permanent remission. It is interesting to wonder what it is about childhood leukemias that make them more responsive to treatment than the adult forms of the disease. Scientists have formulated several related hypotheses to explain this difference. First, many if not most childhood leukemias originate in the fetus. At this early stage of development, the normal cellular controls of cell proliferation and apoptosis are not fully in place. Consequently, the leukemic cells can spread or metastasize in the fetus without having to bypass these normal controls. Therefore the cancer cells are not as abnormal as they would be in adults at the same stage of the disease. Second, because the leukemic cells in a young child never bypassed the apoptosis control, it is possible to trigger cell death by therapeutic means. Third, unlike cancer cells that develop in adults later in life, leukemic cells in young children do not display too much genetic instability or altered genes. Because adult cancers result from the accumulation of many genetic mutations, they can be very difficult to treat. Unlike the situation in childhood leukemias, adult cancer cells have bypassed cell proliferation and apoptosis controls. Finally, because they develop more quickly than adult cancers, leukemic cells in children have little opportunity to develop resistance to treatment.

SUMMARY

Leukemia, the most common form of cancer in children, can occur in patients at birth, throughout childhood, and in adolescence. The symptoms of leukemia in young patients are similar to those experienced by adults: fatigue, swollen spleen, infections, bruising, and bleeding. In addition, metastasis of leukemic cells can produce tumors around the spinal cord, brain, and other sites in the body. The treatment of childhood cancer, particularly ALL, has improved dramatically in recent years. In 1950, almost all children with leukemia died, whereas remission rates are now greater than 90 percent. Unfortunately, some of the treatments can produce undesirable side effects such as secondary tumors. The risk factors and causes of childhood leukemia are not understood fully although scientists are exploring many hypotheses.

6

EXTERNAL RISK FACTORS AND CAUSES OF LEUKEMIA

KEY POINTS

♦ Exposure to high energy radiation is associated with cancer, leukemia in particular.

♦ Exposure to benzene and certain other chemicals is clearly linked to the development of leukemia.

♦ Exposure to herbicides and/or pesticides increases leukemia risk.

♦ Adult T-cell leukemia is caused by infection with the human thymus-derived T-cell leukemia virus (HTLV-1).

LESSONS FROM HIROSHIMA

The United States officially entered World War II in December 1941 after Japan bombed Pearl Harbor. The United States, Great Britain, and the Soviet Union were united in their battle against the spread and domination of Nazism and Fascism in Europe even as the United States and Great Britain fought a second front in the Pacific against the Japanese. In 1945, Germany surrendered unconditionally, thus ending the long European conflict; fighting with Japan continued on the Pacific front. Unfortunately, Japan gave no signs of being willing to surrender even though U.S. aircraft were bombing cities in Japan. A firebomb raid in March 1945 had killed almost 100,000 people and injured more than one million in Tokyo. This city was bombed again in May 1945 and another 83,000 people were killed. In addition, the United States Navy had successfully cut off all supply deliveries to Japan. Nevertheless, military experts generally agreed that the Japanese would never surrender and that ground invasion of the island was going to be necessary to end the war. If such an invasion was to be undertaken, it was certain to be costly in terms of lives lost and people injured. The initial landings of troops were scheduled for the fall and winter of 1945–1946. There were two million Japanese soldiers in Japan and they had approximately 10,000 military aircraft. Given that the campaign to capture the island of Okinawa took more than 10 weeks and resulted in the deaths of more than 12,000 Americans, 100,000 Japanese, and approximately 100,000 native Okinawans, the predicted death toll from an invasion of Japan was ghastly.

Unbeknownst to the Japanese, the United States had been involved in the Manhattan Project, a secret effort to develop an atomic bomb. President Harry Truman made the controversial decision to drop an atomic bomb on Japan with the objective of getting Japan to surrender without the need for a protracted, high-casualty ground force invasion. Historians disagree about whether Truman made the right choice. On August 6, 1945, the United States became the only nation to have used a nuclear weapon in war when a B-29 bomber called the *Enola Gay* dropped a 9,700-pound uranium bomb on the city of Hiroshima. (This was followed on August 9 by the atomic bombing of Nagasaki. Japan surrendered on August 15, 1945.) At the time, the population of Hiroshima was approximately 300,000. The city was a military center and there were about 43,000 soldiers present. The bomb was dropped and it detonated 1,900 feet above the city with a force equivalent to 15,000 tons of dynamite.

The consequences of the bomb were devastating. Within minutes, 90 percent of people within a half-mile radius of the bomb's center were dead. Almost all structures within a mile of the bomb were destroyed and buildings within 3 miles were badly damaged. Terrible fires engulfed the city. Flames destroyed more than 4.4 square miles of the city. At least 70,000 people died from the initial blast. By the end of 1945, the death toll exceeded 100,000 because of aftereffects such as radiation sickness. By 1950, the death toll exceeded 200,000, but one of the worst long-term effects of the bomb was radiation fallout or contamination. This exposure to radiation increased the incidence of cancer, especially leukemia, in populations in and near Hiroshima.[1,2]

EXPOSURE

The association between cancer and radiation was well known long before World War II. In 1902 Albert Frieben, a German scientist, reported that X-rays were carcinogenic. The bombings of Hiroshima and Nagasaki may have ended the war but they also initiated a huge unintended experiment that asked: What happens to a large population of people in the years following exposure to massive levels of radiation? The Hiroshima population received medical help and was monitored very shortly after the blast. The entire exposed population was also monitored every two years thereafter. A paper summarizing the observations of survivors from 1945 to 1958 reported a higher incidence of leukemia among people closest to the epicenter. This higher incidence was evident more than three years after exposure. Moreover, the peak incidence occurred from 1950 to 1952. The relative leukemia incidence diminished but was still higher than that of the general population 13 years after the bomb. Scientists also evaluated the outcomes of exposure to various levels of radiation and found that the higher the radiation dose, the greater the incidence of leukemia. The relationship was linear.[3]

Radiation is believed to increase the likelihood of developing leukemia because it damages DNA and chromosomes. It can take a while for leukemia, or any cancer, to develop after the damage so it is no surprise that leukemia incidence continued to rise even years after the bomb. Scientists also observed that the most prevalent type of leukemia in atomic bomb survivors was CML, which is caused by chromosome breakage and the creation of the Philadelphia chromosome, a genetic change associated with the occurrence of CML.

In addition to the observations of the relationship between radiation and leukemia revealed by the Hiroshima population, scientists have also demonstrated that exposure to radiation therapy for other cancers increases the likelihood of developing leukemia. Therapeutic X-rays to the thyroid region in childhood or *in utero* exposure also increases leukemia incidence. Similarly, in the days before adequate safety measures were taken to protect workers, occupational exposure to high-energy radiation also increased leukemia incidence. For example, radiologists who performed X-ray examinations of patients and people working with radioactive materials in an industrial setting were particularly vulnerable.

SPOTLIGHT ON CANCER SCIENTISTS:
MARIE CURIE (1867–1934)

Winner of two Nobel Prizes, one for Chemistry and one for Physics, Marie Curie is not a name generally associated with cancer research. Although it is true that she did not study medicine or biology directly, Curie's discovery of the radioactive element radium and her development of its applications provided important information about cancer causation, detection, and treatment.

Born in Poland in 1867, Marie Sklodowska was the youngest of five children in a relatively poor family. While still a very young woman, her mother died and her father was not able to support her financially. As a consequence, Marie worked as a governess and helped finance her sister's medical studies. In 1891, it was Marie's turn. She moved to Paris and lived with her sister. Driven to learn, Marie attended Sorbonne University and studied physics and math. In 1894, she met Pierre Curie, another scientist. They married a year later, in 1895, and continued their personal and professional collaboration until his death in 1906.

One of the earliest medical uses of radiation was to treat malignancies. This procedure was called "curie-therapy." Radiation therapy continues to be an essential tool for the treatment of many forms of cancer. Marie Curie also realized that X-rays could be used to see inside the body. When World War I erupted in 1914, Marie Curie, along with her 17-year-old daughter Irene, equipped ambulances with X-ray units and traveled to where injured soldiers were located. Marie Curie reasoned, correctly, that X-ray examination would be a critical help for visualizing broken bones, locating bomb shrapnel or bullets in bodies, and helping make surgeries

Figure 6.1   Marie Curie (seated) with her daughter Irène Joliot-Curie. *(© AP Images)*

more accurate. This pioneering use of X-rays has been extended to the many types of visualization techniques that modern physicians have to see tumors inside the body. Eventually, the long-term exposure to radioactivity revealed one more important fact. High-energy radiation is associated with an increased risk of certain cancers, such as leukemia. Sadly, Marie Curie demonstrated this relationship personally; she died of leukemia in 1934. The family sacrifice did not end there. Marie Curie's daughter Irene, also a Nobel Prize–winning physicist, died of leukemia in 1956. As is true of her mother, Irene's death has been attributed to excessive radiation exposure.

Information about possible risk factors or causes of leukemia, or any cancer, often come from an unintended "experiment" wherein a population of people is exposed to some material and then some time later, maybe even years, public health professionals, physicians, or scientists notice an increase in disease incidence in those who were exposed. Such is the case for the chemicals associated with increased risk of leukemia.

Benzene

Exposure to industrial solvents, especially benzene, is tightly linked to the development of leukemia. In 1928 Delore and Borgomano, two Italian physicians, were the first to report a case of "benzene leukemia" in a person who had been regularly exposed to that chemical in his work. In 1932 Dr. Lignac, a French scientist, did an experiment in which he administered 0.001 milliliters of benzene dissolved in olive oil to 54 white mice. He fed the benzene to the mice weekly for between 17 and 21 weeks. At the end of the experiment, Lignac observed that 6 of the 54 mice had developed leukemia and 2 more had developed lymphoma, a different type of blood cancer. Lignac also had 1,465 control mice to which no benzene had been given; none of these animals developed leukemia.[4] Lignac was able to show experimentally what had been suspected from retroactive studies of people: Benzene dramatically increased the likelihood of leukemia.

Because benzene was used liberally in manufacturing, leather working, and metal engraving, exposure was a serious problem affecting many workers in the early twentieth century. For the people working in this wide range of industries, exposure to benzene was the only commonality, and they developed leukemia at rates much higher than the general population. For example, a 36-year-old woman working from 1942 to 1964 as a finisher of electric cables, used benzene to clear the rubber covering for the wires and died of leukemia in 1967. Similarly, a 37-year-old woman, who worked from 1959 to 1966 in a beauty case factory, assembled the case by spreading the benzene-containing glue with her finger over the lining of the case. She also died of leukemia in 1967. In a third case, a 31-year-old man, who worked as a shoemaker from 1959 to 1961, had to shape the toes of the shoes by softening the leather with 40 percent benzene. He died of leukemia in 1965.[5]

It is clear that the association between benzene exposure and leukemia development is a strong one. Nevertheless, as is true for most carcinogens, there can be a time lag of years between exposure and the onset of the disease. With benzene and leukemia, the lag is anywhere from 3 years to more than 20 years. Workers exposed to benzene often exhibit chromosomal damage, and because leukemia is caused by an accumulation of errors in DNA, the time it takes after exposure for the damage to occur influences how quickly a person develops leukemia.

Pesticides and Herbicides

The other principal categories of chemicals associated with leukemia are herbicides and pesticides. The majority of more than 30 studies in the medical literature show an association between adult leukemias and farming and/or herbicide/pesticide exposure. For example, the phenoxy herbicides, used to kill leaf weeds, are linked to CLL. The increased leukemia risk in those exposed is not dramatically higher than that of the general population—no more than approximately 1.5 times greater. However, concern about these environmental chemicals is intense because, as with radiation, the most vulnerable individuals are children.

Figure 6.2   Benzene was once a common chemical used in making leather items, such as shoes. Exposure to benzene can cause chromosomal damage that can cause a cancer such as leukemia to form. (© http://www.vittorebuzzi.it /Alamy)

Besides benzene, pesticides, and herbicides, scientists believe that exposure to certain other **volatile solvents** that damage bone marrow increases the risk of leukemia. Volatile solvents are chemicals that evaporate into a gaseous form at room temperature. For example, formaldehyde, a chemical that is sometimes used as a preservative, is associated with leukemia. Finally, chemotherapy drugs used to treat other cancers, chemicals that alter DNA structure, chemicals that prevent DNA repair, and tobacco smoke all increase the risk of leukemia, probably by damaging the blood stem cells of the bone marrow.

INFECTION

The experimental and intellectual path to the understanding that some cancers, including a certain type of leukemia, are caused by infection was a long and tortuous one. In 1908 the Danish scientists Vilhelm Ellerman and Oluf Bang showed that a virus caused chicken leukemia. The scientific community did not think that this discovery was particularly important. After all, the reasoning went, chickens are not at all like humans, so this finding is irrelevant. Also, in 1908, scientists and physicians did not fully understand that leukemia was a blood cancer. Because solid tumors do not form in leukemia, this disease did not resemble the cancers with which physicians were more familiar.

Ironically, the next big breakthrough was another observation made in chicken. In 1911 the American scientist Peyton Rous demonstrated that sarcoma, a muscle tumor, was caused by a virus. The **Rous sarcoma virus (RSV)** was the first of many tumor viruses that scientists discovered. Again, the scientific community was underwhelmed by this amazing finding. Eventually, Rous was vindicated. Other cancer researchers finally caught up with Rous, and he was awarded the Nobel Prize for Medicine or Physiology in 1966.

What other pieces of evidence needed to be put in place for scientists to accept the hypothesis that some cancers are caused by infection, especially by tumor-causing viruses? First, in the 1930s, two **oncogenic**, or cancer-causing, viruses were observed in mammals. The Shope papilloma virus was shown to produce large skin tumors, especially on the head. Similarly, John Bittner discovered a factor present in mouse milk that can cause mammary tumors. This factor is the Bittner virus. Although leukemia was recognized as a cancer during the late nineteenth century, it was not until 1951 that Ludwik Gross showed leukemia in mice was caused by a virus. In fact, between 1951

SPOTLIGHT ON CANCER SCIENTISTS:
JOHANNES FIBIGER (1867–1928)

Winner of the Nobel Prize for Physiology or Medicine in 1926, Johannes Fibiger's work is barely described in the information disseminated about him by the Nobel Foundation. Perhaps the reason for this reticence is because his Nobel Prize–winning discovery could never be replicated by other scientists.

Fibiger observed that in three cases of spontaneous gastric, or stomach, cancer in wild rats, a nematode worm was present in the gut too. He named this worm *Spiroptera carcinoma* and studied its life cycle. Fibiger learned that the cockroach was the intermediate host for the worm. Armed with this knowledge, he infected cockroaches with *S. carcinoma* and fed the infected insects to laboratory rats. Of 62 rats that survived for more

and 1972, 26 mammalian oncogenic viruses could be visualized using an **electron microscope**. Finally scientists could see that these infections were caused by discrete particles that had a physical basis. In 1975 David Baltimore was awarded the Nobel Prize for demonstrating that tumor viruses physically interact with the cell's genes. As with radiation, viruses produce cancer by damaging or altering DNA structure and/or function.

Given that more than 15 percent of cancers worldwide are probably due to infection, it is startling that it took so long for the scientific community to accept this reality. In the case of leukemia, one particular form, adult T-cell leukemia, is caused by human thymus-derived T-cell leukemia virus (HTLV-1).

than 60 days, 12 developed stomach cancer. Interestingly, the worms and their eggs were present in the primary tumors but not on the secondary tumors that resulted from metastasis. Fibiger concluded that *S. carcinoma* caused stomach cancer. He published this work in 1913.

Despite many efforts, no one could duplicate these findings. Fibiger died in 1928 shortly before other scientists demonstrated that the rats had developed cancers because of a lack of nutrition. Evidently, the worms played no part in the story after all. It is particularly ironic that Fibiger's Nobel Prize in 1926 was the first one awarded in the field of the infectious causes of cancer. When evidence did emerge that some cancers are indeed caused by infectious agents, especially certain types of viruses, the scientific community ignored these results for a long time probably because the idea of an infectious cause for cancer had been so embarrassingly discredited.

HTLV-1 is an example of a **retrovirus**. Instead of containing DNA as their genetic material, retroviruses use RNA. When a host cell is infected, the viral RNA enters the cell and takes over its biochemical machinery.

◆ FELINE LEUKEMIA

Humans are not the only mammals that can develop leukemia; cats can too. Unlike most forms of human leukemia, feline leukemia is caused by a virus, FeLV. In the United States alone, approximately 2 to 3 percent of all cats are infected. The disease spreads when fluids, such as saliva, pass from an infected cat to another cat. FeLV can spread from litter boxes, water or food bowls, and bedding in addition to cat-to-cat contact. Kittens are much more susceptible to infections than are adult cats. In fact, the amount of virus needed to infect 100 percent of a population of kittens would infect no more than 30 percent of a similarly sized population of adult cats.

Feline leukemia is a potentially fatal disease. Approximately 20 percent of infected cats will die. Because the immune system is severely weakened, affected cats are likely to suffer from infections. Some cats with feline leukemia develop solid tumors and severe anemia.

Although FeLV does not infect humans, the other diseases that cats develop because of feline leukemia could definitely put young, elderly, or immunocompromised individuals at risk. Consequently, people should avoid exposure to infected cats.

There is no cure for feline leukemia. Treatments are aimed at relieving pain and suffering. The best approach is prevention by vaccination and keeping cats indoors and away from infected cats.

The virus makes a DNA copy of its RNA **genome**. This "viral RNA" inserts itself randomly into the host cell's DNA. HTLV-1 targets T-cells, makes them immortal, and triggers cell proliferation. Since those cells will not die, even if apoptosis is signaled, they can continue to divide. The cells that are produced do not function normally and, as with other types of leukemia, they will crowd out healthy cells.

The incidence of the HTLV-1 infection is not the same all over the world. Prevalence is highest in southwestern Japan, the Caribbean Islands, South America, Central Africa, Papua New Guinea, and the Solomon Islands. Approximately 5 to 15 percent of adults are infected in these locales. Transmission of HTLV-1 is by bodily fluids. Infection is usually acquired in infancy by nursing infected milk. Infection can also be spread by sexual contact, blood transfusions, or the sharing of contaminated hypodermic needles. HTLV-1 causes leukemia in a high percentage of the people it infects. Its genetic material contains instructions that enable it to bind to T-cells and activate host genes that trigger cell division (even in the absence of growth factors) as well as block host inhibitors of cell division.

SUMMARY

There is no single cause for all types or cases of leukemia. Known risk factors include exposure to high-energy radiation, benzene and certain other chemical solvents, pesticides, and, in the case of adult T-cell leukemia, the retrovirus HTLV-1. Most cases of leukemia cannot, however, be linked to specific, identifiable risk factors.

7

INTERNAL RESPONSES TO RISK FACTORS: GENES AND CHROMOSOME CHANGES

KEY POINTS

♦ Genetic disorders that affect bone marrow also increase the likelihood of developing leukemia.

♦ There are several specific oncogenes that are involved in the development of leukemia.

♦ Dysfunctional tumor suppressor genes increase the risk of leukemia.

♦ The Philadelphia chromosome, produced by a translocation, is associated with the development of chronic myelogenous leukemia.

Leukemia, like other cancers, is a genetic disease. Mistakes, defects, and malfunctions occur in genes and/or chromosomes. If enough errors accumulate in the genes that are important for the regulation of cell communication, cell division, DNA repair, apoptosis, and differentiation, a cell becomes cancerous. Scientists have accumulated a vast amount of evidence showing that gene and chromosome dysfunction can lead to leukemia. Let's consider some of what they have learned.

OTHER DISEASES THAT INCREASE LEUKEMIA RISK

If the development of leukemia is indeed related to genetic malfunctions in blood-forming cells, one might expect that inherited genetic disorders that affect bone marrow and/or cell division might have an impact on the development of leukemia. This prediction is borne out in several diseases. Fanconi's anemia, an inherited disease that leads to bone marrow failure, increases the likelihood of leukemia. Similarly, **Schwachman-Diamond syndrome**, another inherited disease, is responsible not only for an insufficiently functioning **pancreas**, but also for dysfunctional bone marrow and the consequent increased risk of leukemia. **Bloom syndrome** is another inherited disorder in which a gene mutation leads to excessive chromosome breakage. Individuals with Bloom syndrome suffer from growth deficiencies both before and after they are born, mental retardation, and extreme sensitivity to light. Also, they have an increased risk of leukemia. Li-Fraumeni syndrome is linked to the development of many types of cancer, including leukemia. In this disease, individuals inherit a mutated version of the tumor suppressor gene. Individuals with **ataxia telangiectasia**, an inherited immunodeficiency disease, have an increased likelihood of developing leukemia because the mutated gene interferes with the normal cellular mechanisms that prevent damaged DNA from replicating. When defective DNA replicates, errors accumulate even more rapidly. Finally, individuals with Down syndrome are also at an increased risk of leukemia. The genetic mistake in Down syndrome is the presence of an extra chromosome 21. Instead of possessing only 2 copies of chromosome 21, cells of Down syndrome patients have three; Down syndrome is also called trisomy-21. Scientists are not certain why Down syndrome increases leukemia risk but they speculate that the chromosomes might be more fragile and vulnerable to breakage.

It is interesting that there is such a broad array of genetic diseases that increase the likelihood of leukemia. The only thing that all of these disorders appear to have in common is that they possess defective or malfunctioning versions of genes that are important for blood cell division, development, and differentiation. Most leukemias occur, however, in the absence of any particular inherited disease. Nevertheless, these leukemias also involve altered or dysfunctional genes. Several external factors can trigger the development of leukemia, including high-energy radiation, chemotherapy, exposure to benzene and certain other chemicals, diet, and HTLV-1. All of these causative agents also have one thing in common: They damage genes and/or chromosomes, thus increasing the leukemia risk. A person can inherit a disease that has the capacity to assault gene structure and function, and he or she can be exposed to external factors that can do the same type of genetic damage. What genes are important for regulating division in blood-forming cells?

ONCOGENES AND LEUKEMIA

Peyton Rous' discovery of a tumor-causing virus, though not fully understood or appreciated until decades later, was actually the first of many steps in the research path that led to our understanding of oncogenes and proto-oncogenes. The Rous sarcoma virus (RSV) possesses an oncogene called *src,* which is an altered form of a normal cellular gene, or proto-oncogene. When cells are infected with RSV, the *src* oncogene produces an abnormal protein that tells the cell to undergo division. This activation of cell division cannot be turned off because the defective *src* protein will not respond to normal cellular signals trying to stop it. As a consequence, the infected cells become cancerous.

Although oncogenes were first revealed by studying tumor-causing viruses, most oncogenes are not introduced into human cells by infection. In fact, oncogenes generally originate from a normal cellular gene that has been altered with respect to its structure and/or function. The proteins encoded by proto-oncogenes play critical roles in the elaborate, carefully orchestrated biochemical pathways that regulate cell communication, division, survival, and differentiation. When a proto-oncogene is changed to an oncogene, often due to factors that damage or alter DNA, a component of one of these pathways gets stuck "on." If enough oncogenes are present, the cumulative errors will produce cancer.

Let's consider the general logic of those biochemical pathways and how the **transformation** from proto-oncogenes to oncogenes can lead to cancer. First, cells communicate whether or not to undergo division by producing chemical signals called growth factors. Normally growth factor production and release are carefully regulated. If oncogenes ensure that growth factors are continually present, cells will be signaled constantly to divide. Second, growth factors ordinarily bind to and activate receptors present in the cell membrane. When the growth factor is bound to the receptor, a signal is sent to the cell's interior indicating that cell division should occur. An oncogene that produces an altered receptor can remain activated even in the absence of a growth factor. Uncontrolled cell division can result. Third, an activated receptor triggers the production of signaling molecules inside the cell. These molecules activate a cascade of additional **signal molecules**—think of a "bucket brigade"—that ultimately reach gene regulatory molecules in the nucleus. The end point of this entire communication pathway resides at the genes. Regulatory molecules control which genes are "on" and which are "off." Oncogenes that perpetually produce any of these cellular-signaling molecules will activate the pathway leading to cell division. Oncogenes that produce altered gene regulatory proteins can activate and deactivate genes in a manner that keeps cells dividing. There are also proto-oncogenes that encode for normal proteins whose jobs are to repair damaged DNA, trigger apoptosis, or promote differentiation. When these proto-oncogenes are transformed into oncogenes, DNA errors cannot be fixed, damaged cells do not undergo apoptosis, and cells remain in a perpetually dividing, undifferentiated state.

Scientists have identified several specific oncogenes that play roles in the development of leukemia. For example, *v-erb-b,* which is found in chickens, and the human oncogenes *abl, PML/RAR* alpha, and *PDGFR,* encode for receptors that continually signal bone marrow cells to divide even in the absence of an appropriate signal. A similar oncogene that affects receptors, *v-mpl,* is important in mouse leukemia. The human oncogenes *K-RAS* and *TEL-JAK2* each produce intracellular signal molecules that continue the pathway of communication even under inappropriate conditions. Finally, the oncogene *c-myc,* found in chickens, encodes a transcription factor that regulates gene expression such that cell proliferation is activated.

TUMOR SUPPRESSOR GENES AND LEUKEMIA

While proto-oncogenes are responsible for encoding proteins that encourage cell proliferation, survival, and differentiation when conditions

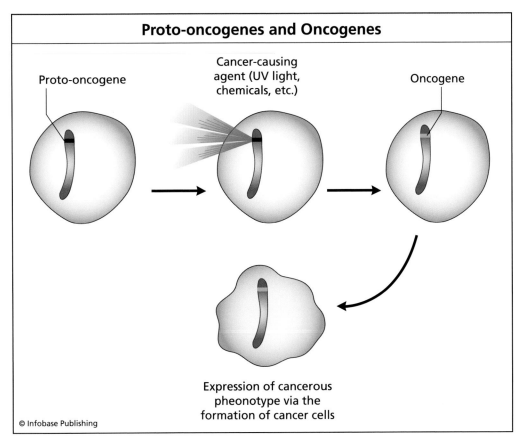

Proto-oncogenes and Oncogenes

Proto-oncogene

Cancer-causing agent (UV light, chemicals, etc.)

Oncogene

Expression of cancerous pheonotype via the formation of cancer cells

© Infobase Publishing

Figure 7.1   Proto-oncogenes can be transformed into oncogenes when they are exposed to certain agents that affect their DNA. These agents might be radiation, UV light, or certain chemicals. Oncogenes can activate the formation of cancer cells.

are appropriate, tumor suppressor genes put the brakes on these processes when necessary. If the DNA of a cell is damaged or if the cell is not prepared to divide, the proteins produced thanks to the tumor suppressor genes halt the march toward cell proliferation. If the cell needs to make additional materials so that division can proceed, or if DNA must be repaired, tumor suppressor proteins will delay cell division.

If a cell or its DNA is too damaged to repair, tumor suppressor proteins will trigger apoptosis. In this way, mutated genes are not passed on to a new generation of cells. Proto-oncogenes and tumor suppressor genes work together in a carefully balanced way to assure that cell proliferation is tightly regulated.

When proto-oncogenes are transformed into oncogenes, the "go" signal is delivered permanently. If tumor suppressor genes are functional, their "stop" signal can often override the information from the oncogene. However, if tumor suppressor genes are mutated or altered, this critical stop signal disappears. Scientists have observed that tumor suppressor genes are lost, inactivated, or dysfunctional in most, if not all, cancers.

As in the case for oncogenes, scientists have identified several specific tumor suppressor genes important in leukemia. For example, *p53*, a human tumor suppressor gene, encodes for a protein that together with some other molecules is able to assess DNA and chromosome damage. The *p53* protein is a transcription factor: it regulates whether specific genes are actively directing the synthesis of other proteins. When DNA is damaged, *p53* delays cell division and regulates the genes involved in repair. Once the DNA has been corrected, cell division can resume. If DNA damage is so great that it cannot be repaired, *p53* triggers apoptosis. It is easy to see how a loss of normal *p53* can lead cells to proliferate uncontrollably. In fact, *p53* is lost or dysfunctional in 50 percent of all human cancers.[1,2,3] In addition to the tumor suppressor gene *p53, INK4* is also important in leukemia. This tumor suppressor normally inhibits cell division directly and it also stabilizes *p53* protein in the cell. Loss of *INK4* function contributes to the development of leukemia and certain other cancers.

THE PHILADELPHIA CHROMOSOME

The idea that chromosomes, the structures in the cell's nucleus and the physical repository of genes, might be important in cancer development dates back to the nineteenth century. The German scientist David von Hanseman examined cancer cells with a microscope and observed chromosomal abnormalities that he did not see in normal cells; he

---

SPOTLIGHT ON CANCER SCIENTISTS:
SIR DAVID LANE, PH.D. (1951-)

In 1978 David Lane published a paper that changed the future of cancer research. In it, he described the protein *p53*, a molecule that plays a critical role in both aging and cancer. Mutations in the gene that encodes *p53* are present in at least 50 percent of all cancers. Known as the "guardian of the genome," *p53* is a tumor suppressor. When the DNA of a cell is damaged or if the cell starts to divide uncontrollably, the level of *p53* protein rises in the cell. As a consequence, cell division is halted and, if possible, DNA is repaired. If the DNA damage is too great, the cell is directed to undergo apoptosis. In cases where the *p53* gene is mutated, cell division is not stopped and a tumor forms.

Dr. Lane was born in England in 1951. He attended University College London, receiving his bachelor's degree in 1973 and his Ph.D. in 1976. He is presently a professor of surgery and oncology at the University of Dundee in Scotland. David Lane was knighted in 2000 for his contributions to our understanding of cancer.

published his findings in 1890. In the early twentieth century Theodor Boveri, a German embryologist, extended this work and in 1914 published *The Origin of Malignant Tumors.* Boveri speculated that the "predominance" of chromosomes that promote cell division or the absence of chromosomes that inhibit proliferation was responsible for cancer. His hypothesis was amazingly prescient, particularly because in 1914 no one had any knowledge of the physical structure of genes, DNA, or gene expression, let alone tumor suppressors or oncogenes. Of course, Boveri was correct. Chromosomes do play an essential role in cancer formation. In fact, the first evidence that a chromosome abnormality could be a cause, rather than an effect, of cancer was in the case of chronic myelogenous leukemia and the Philadelphia chromosome.

In 1956 Dr. Peter Nowell was a young assistant professor and scientist working at the University of Pennsylvania. He and his graduate student David Hungerford were studying CML. Interested in what was going wrong in the cells of CML patients, they collected blood, grew the cells on microscopic slides, and stained the cells with dyes in order to visualize the chromosomes. Nowell and Hungerford carefully made detailed observations of many samples. They wanted to see whether CML cells had any changes in the number, size, or shape of chromosomes compared to what they saw in normal cells. Their painstaking work paid off—in 1960 they identified an unusual small chromosome in the leukemia cells of a CML patient.[4,5] In fact, Nowell and Hungerford found this structure, which they named the Philadelphia chromosome after the city in which it was discovered, in the leukemic cells of other CML patients but never in normal cells. Their discovery turned out to be of wide-ranging importance; the Philadelphia chromosome is a specific example of a more general phenomenon. In all, there are more than 200

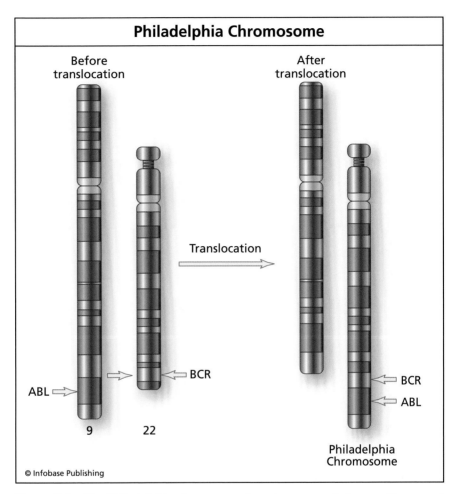

Philadelphia Chromosome

Before translocation

After translocation

Translocation

ABL

BCR

9   22

BCR

ABL

Philadelphia Chromosome

© Infobase Publishing

Figure 7.2   The Philadelphia chromosome is a chromosomal abnormality caused by the translocation of genetic material in chromosomes 9 and 22. In 1960 the Philadelphia chromosome was linked to chronic myelogenous leukemia.

chromosomal abnormalities that are associated with particular types of cancer, especially leukemia.

When Nowell and Hungerford were doing their experiments, techniques and methods had not yet been invented to determine exactly what had changed structurally in the chromosome and how function was affected. Ultimately, over the course of decades, several teams of scientists studying the Philadelphia chromosome and its relationship to CML learned exactly what chromosome and genes are involved and why leukemia develops.

Sometimes chromosomes can break, and when they do the broken ends are "sticky," meaning that they bind readily to another broken end.

SPOTLIGHT ON CANCER SCIENTISTS:
PETER NOWELL, M.D. (1928–)

When Peter Nowell began his medical research career, almost nothing was known about cancer genetics. Yet he and his colleague, David Hungerford, discovered the first definite relationship between a genetic change and the development of cancer, and in doing so, originated the field of cancer cytogenetics.

Peter Nowell was born in Philadelphia and has rarely lived away from his hometown. He earned his bachelor's degree from Wesleyan University in Connecticut and then returned to Philadelphia to attend medical school at the University of Pennsylvania. After his residency training and two years at the United States Naval Radiological Defense Laboratory, Nowell joined the pathology department at the University of Pennsylvania in 1956. He has been there ever since.

Nowell first developed an interest in leukemia during his residency. When he began his job at the University of Pennsylvania, he decided to continue the studies he had begun at the United States Naval Radiological Defense Laboratory. He grew human leukemic cells on microscope

Chromosome breakage can be caused by several external factors including exposure to high doses of radiation. In the case of CML, a piece of chromosome 9 detaches and sticks to the broken end of chromosome 22. This **translocation** event occurs in bone marrow stem cells and therefore is present in all cells derived from these cells. When this chromosome translocation occurs, some of the genes on chromosomes

slides and stained them with a dye so that chromosomes could be visualized and identified. Working with a graduate student, David Hungerford, Nowell examined the blood cells of individuals who suffered from acute or chronic leukemias. They discovered that the white blood cells of patients with chronic myelogenous leukemia (CML) possessed an odd, tiny chromosome not present in normal cells. Nowell and Hungerford reasoned, correctly, that this chromosome was due to genetic change that had occurred in a single cell and that all of the offspring of this cell also had this alteration. Moreover, they realized that this abnormal chromosome, called the Philadelphia chromosome, was the cause of CML, not a response to the disease. They published their findings in 1960 but it was not until the development of molecular biological techniques in the 1980s that scientists were able to determine exactly what happened at the level of the DNA.

Peter Nowell was and remains a cheerful man with a good sense of humor. Not self-important in any way, he seems surprised by the many awards he has collected, all starting from what he calls his "stumbling" across the Philadelphia chromosome.

9 and 22 are repositioned. Specifically, the proto-oncogene *abl* from chromosome 9 winds up next to *bcr* (breakpoint cluster region) on chromosome 22. One of the products of this translocation is a shortened chromosome 22 (the Philadelphia chromosome), and the other is a lengthened chromosome 9. The *abl* proto-oncogene is not translocated in its entirety, however, and as a result it is transformed into an onco-gene. The two genes, *bcr* and *abl,* are fused and produce an abnormal fusion protein. The normal *abl* gene encodes for a receptor that signals cell divisions if growth factor is bound to it. The fusion *bcr-abl* protein is a dysfunctional receptor. It permanently signals cell proliferation even in the absence of growth factors.

Ninety-five percent of all CML patients exhibit the Philadelphia chro-mosome. While the drug Gleevec successfully inhibits the oncogenic protein produced by the fused *bcr-abl* gene, producing a 96 percent rate of remission in the early phases of CML, the only cure is a bone marrow transplant. The presence of the Philadelphia chromosome is necessary but not sufficient for CML to progress to the more serious blast phase. For this event to occur, tumor suppressor genes must be lost or mutated. Alterations in *p53* have been observed in 30 percent of blast crisis cells, and in another 20 percent the tumor suppressor *Rb1* is affected. These defects in tumor suppressor genes have not been observed in chronic phase CML or normal cells.[6] Evidently, tumor sup-pressor gene defects have a role in the progression of CML but not in the initiation of the disease. Finally, the Philadelphia chromosome is also seen in a subset of patients with ALL or AML. The prognosis is poor for these patients compared to individuals who do not exhibit the Philadelphia chromosome.

SUMMARY

Leukemia, like any cancer, is a genetic disease in the sense that an accumulation of specific gene mutations is necessary for a cell to become fully malignant. Some of the types of genes that are important for the development of leukemia are oncogenes and tumor suppressors. Oncogenes originate from normal cellular genes, called proto-oncogenes, which were damaged or changed. Instead of following normal growth controls, oncogenes continually encourage cell division. Tumor suppressor genes control, slow, and if appropriate, stop cell proliferation. When tumor suppressor genes are lost or damaged, their ability to regulate cell division disappears. Finally, the genetic change associated with the development of leukemia can involve the rearrangement of entire chromosomes, as is the case for the Philadelphia chromosome and CML.

8

DIAGNOSIS, TREATMENT, AND PREVENTION OF LEUKEMIA

KEY POINTS

- Leukemia is diagnosed after a physical exam followed by blood test and a bone marrow biopsy.

- The principal treatment for leukemia is chemotherapy although radiation therapy is used in some circumstances.

- Chemotherapy often produces side-effects including hair loss, nausea, and fatigue.

- Stem cell transplantation is the only method with the potential to cure leukemia.

- Stem cell transplantation sometimes produces side effects, the most serious of which is graft-versus-host disease.

- Future treatments include the development of new chemotherapy drugs and improved stem cell transplantation therapies.

Cammy Lee's life changed completely in 1986. She was 13 years old, enjoying the start of her teen years, when, like a bolt out of the blue, she was diagnosed with ALL. The prognosis was not as positive as Cammy and her family hoped because her ALL was accompanied by the presence of the Philadelphia chromosome. As her physicians explained, this extra problem made Cammy's treatment more challenging. Since her leukemia was an acute rather than a chronic form, treatment began immediately. Cammy underwent radiation therapy and extensive chemotherapy. In fact, she had to undergo many rounds of treatment because her leukemia would not remain in remission. By 1992 Cammy's had experienced two **relapses***, meaning the return of her leukemia. Her physicians indicated that Cammy's last chance to survive was a bone marrow transplant.*

Ordinarily, physicians look to biologically related family members for bone marrow donations. There is generally a 20 percent chance of a good bone marrow match between siblings. If the match is not a good one, the recipient's body can reject the transplantation. Cammy had five siblings so everyone assumed that at least one would be a suitable donor. Unfortunately none of her siblings was a match.

Next, Cammy's family and physicians turned to the National Marrow Donor Program. There are more than 1.2 million volunteer donors in the registry but only about 3 percent of them were Asian (like Cammy). It is important to match, as much as possible, the ethnicity of the donor and recipient because it increases the likelihood that the cells of both individuals have similar proteins on their surfaces, thereby reducing the risk of rejection. The odds were very much against Cammy. Given the small percentage of the donor population that would be suitable for her to search, the chance of finding a suitable donor was close to zero.

Cammy's family did not give up. Instead, they saw this setback as an opportunity to help not only Cammy, but others in her situation as well.

They searched for donors beyond the National Marrow Donor Program. In fact, they actually began to recruit donors for an organization they created called the Cammy Lee Leukemia Foundation (CLLF). Their work and determination paid off; in 1992 Cammy found a match. Virginia Lau, a Chinese-Canadian mother of three, saved Cammy's life by donating bone marrow.

Cammy and Virginia met in 1994. Cammy resolved to live her life fully and meaningfully. She graduated from Rutgers University in 1999. She works full time as the recruitment manager for the CLLF. Her efforts, and those of her colleagues, have been amazingly successful. Since the start of the foundation, more than 100,000 minority donors have been registered in the National Marrow Donor Program, thus giving hope and a chance to a wider array of people than ever before.[1]

HOW IS LEUKEMIA DIAGNOSED?

Once a patient is suspected of having leukemia, further tests and other diagnostic methods are undertaken to determine whether that person has leukemia, and if so, what type of leukemia and what treatments to begin.

The first clues that something is wrong include fatigue that will not go away; a greater than ordinary frequency of colds and other infections; and swelling in the left side of the abdomen where the spleen is located, or in lymph nodes. There are many possible causes for this array of symptoms, most of them not serious, but a physician would probably order tests to see if leukemia is the problem.

The first tests would examine the blood cell population in the patient's body. The physician or nurse collects a blood sample, which is examined by **medical technologists**. The blood will be examined microscopically as well as through the process of **flow cytometry**, which separates the cells into different groups. In this way, the number of red blood cells and each of the types of leukocytes can be determined. Flow cytometry enables the technologist to determine whether the number of each type of blood cell is in the healthy range or if there is a deficit or overabundance of a particular cell type. If there is an excess of leukocytes, as one would see in leukemia, immunophenotyping is done. This test takes advantage of the fact that different types of leukocytes vary with respect to the specific proteins present in their cell membranes. Identifying exactly which kind of leukocyte is producing leukemic cells is essential for accurate diagnosis as well as for planning treatment.

In addition to determining blood cell counts and identifying the affected cells, physicians also need information about the genes and chromosomes in the leukemic cells. The prognosis and treatment plan for an individual depends on the degree of genetic change that is present. Lots of chromosome damage or gene rearrangement indicates a more troubling prognosis. Medical technologists use cytogenetics and a method called **fluorescence *in situ* hybridization (FISH)** to examine the cells. With cytogenetics, technologists attach leukemic cells to slides, stain them with dyes, and examine the chromosomes to see if the number, shapes, or sizes are different from what they observe in normal cells. FISH is a technique in which chromosomes are stained with a series of differently colored dyes, thus producing a striped pattern. Technologists compare the color pattern in leukemic cell chromosomes with that of normal cell chromosomes to see whether any genes have changed position.

Although physicians can learn a great deal from these blood tests, the final piece of information they need to confirm a diagnosis of leukemia is found in the bone marrow. Unlike blood collection, taking a bone marrow sample is a somewhat complicated and uncomfort-able process. Because it is a painful procedure, the physician uses an anesthetic to numb the location from which bone marrow will be collected. There are two methods available for collecting bone mar-row. With **aspiration**, a relatively fine needle is inserted into a large bone in order to remove some marrow. A method similar to aspiration is used to collect large amounts of marrow. The physician inserts a very thick needle into a large bone and removes both marrow and some bone. Once the marrow is collected, the cells are examined with the same methods used to evaluate blood samples. As is the case for the blood tests, physicians need to know what cells are affected in the bone marrow so they can establish an accurate diagnosis, prognosis, and treatment plan.

HOW IS LEUKEMIA TREATED?

Physicians attack most cancers with one or a combination of the follow-ing: surgery, radiation therapy, or chemotherapy. The goal of treatment is to remove cancer cells and to kill any cancer cells that might remain. In the case of leukemia, surgery is generally not an option because blood cancers are more diffuse throughout the entire body than solid tumors. Blood cancers cannot easily be "removed." Although radiation therapy is often used with other treatments, chemotherapy is by far the primary tool used to fight leukemia. For some cases, chemotherapy provides only temporary remission. Fortunately, many leukemia patients have one more option that offers the potential for a cure—stem cell transplan-tation. In the sections that follow, we will consider these treatments in more detail, as well as their possible side effects and some new avenues for therapy that are being developed.

Radiation

The first clinical radiologists used their arms to determine the appropriate dose for patient therapy. They defined the **erythema dose**, the radiation exposure required to produce pink skin that resembles but is slightly less than a sunburn. Unfortunately, due to their repeated unprotected exposure to radiation, these radiologists developed leukemia at a frequency much higher than the general population.

In the early twentieth century, radiation was the treatment of choice for leukemia. A case from 1930 describes a 60-year-old man with CML who was given 10 series of radiation treatments over a period of two-and-a-half years. He received two-thirds of an erythema dose delivered over his spleen every three months.[2]

Radiation therapy now used to treat leukemia is more refined. A patient may receive radiation on the whole body or directed at the brain, spleen, or other area of the body where leukemia cells have collected and formed a tumor. External beam radiation, a commonly used form of radiation therapy to treat leukemia, aims a high-energy X-ray to the site of a tumor, thus killing the cancer cells. Generally, radiation therapy is done daily, five days a week, for six to eight weeks. Although the treatment itself is painless, potential side effects include fatigue and red, dry, tender skin at the sites of exposure.

Chemotherapy

The ancient Egyptians treated superficial skin lesions, including cancers, with caustic arsenic pastes. The strategy of this therapy is similar to that of radiation therapy—kill the abnormal cells. This method of treating skin cancers persisted into the twentieth century.

The observation that arsenic could eliminate skin cancers led scientists to ask whether other cancers might be treated with similar success.

In 1865 Heinrich Lissauer, a German physician, demonstrated that administering arsenous tri-oxide in the form of a topical medication called Fowler's solution eliminated leukemia in his patients. In 1878 scientists described the response of patients' leukocytes to Fowler's solution. In one case, the leukocyte counts approached normal levels in a patient treated for 10 weeks. When administration of Fowler's solution was stopped, the leukocyte count rose to abnormal levels. When Fowler's solution was once again given to the patient, the leukocyte number went down. A larger study of 10 patients suffering from CML was done at the Boston City Hospital in 1931. Of the 10, nine responded to arsenic trioxide treatment. Their leukocyte counts became normal, enlarged spleens shrunk to normal size, normal blood cell development resumed in the bone marrow, and the patients experienced a sense of well-being. When the arsenic trioxide therapy was discontinued, they all relapsed within weeks. Unfortunately, the majority of the patients ultimately experienced chronic arsenic poisoning.[3] Nevertheless, Fowler's solution became the primary therapy for CML until it was replaced by radiation and other chemotherapy drugs.

Arsenic therapy declined dramatically in the early twentieth century. Amazingly, this treatment of leukemia experienced a rebirth in China in the 1970s. Physicians have been using arsenic trioxide as one aspect of treatment for APL, a subtype of AML. This new, lower-dose version of arsenic therapy is safe and very effective for all stages of APL. Scientists studying the mechanism of arsenic action have demonstrated that this therapy inhibits cell proliferation and encourages apoptosis in leukemic cells.

Arsenic trioxide is certainly an effective component for treating APL, whereas other types of chemotherapy drugs are used for different leukemias. In fact, the type of medication used depends on the specific

◆ ARSENIC: POISON OR CURE?

Long associated with poisoning, both accidental and deliberate, arsenic has also been used throughout history to treat various ailments. Although a large dose is inevitably fatal, smaller amounts of arsenic produce tissue inflammation but not serious illness. When applied externally to the skin, arsenic kills surface cells. A sore forms, and when it sloughs off presumably healthy cells underneath become visible. In this way, arsenic has been used to treat skin ailments, including cancers.

In addition to external use, arsenic was also commonly used in a tonic form called Fowler's solution. People claimed that Fowler's solution could treat various diseases including epilepsy and headaches. **Dermatologists** through the 1960s continued to recommend the external use of Fowler's solution for the treatment of **psoriasis**, a skin inflammation condition. It is important to realize that long-term exposure to even small quantities of arsenic can result in serious side effects such as hair loss, digestive system distress, inflammation of the body's mucous membranes, and problems with the heart and circulatory system. Interestingly, arsenic has returned to the modern pharmacy. In 2000 the FDA approved Trisenox, an arsenic compound, to treat individuals with acute promyelocytic leukemia (APL).

leukemia. Generally, chemotherapy interferes with some aspect of cell division or survival. The idea is to target leukemic cells, although other dividing cell populations in the body are also affected. These populations include hair follicles, the cellular lining of the digestive system, and, in males, developing sperm. As a consequence, some forms of chemotherapy produce side effects such as hair loss, nausea, and loss of fertility. The hair loss and nausea are temporary, and the nausea can be treated. The loss of fertility may or may not be permanent.

Chemotherapy is administered to the patient in various ways, depending on the drugs being used. Some medicines can be swallowed but others need to be delivered intravenously directly into a blood vessel. Some patients receive their drugs through a **catheter**, or tube, placed in a large vein, and other have drugs injected directly into the spinal fluid. Chemotherapy drugs need to reach the brain and spinal cord if leukemic cells are present there; although spinal injection works in many cases, children and even adults sometimes use an **Ommaya reservoir**. This device is a special type of catheter that can be placed under the scalp so drugs can be delivered directly to the brain.

There are more than 50 different types of chemotherapeutic agents that are used alone and in various combinations to treat leukemia. Many of these drugs stop leukemic cells from dividing by interfering with their DNA. Others attack specific proteins that the leukemic cells need to live, or to divide. Examples of three newer treatments that are more specialized for particular leukemias are imatinib mesylate (Gleevec), tretinoin (Vesanoid), and gemtuzumab ozogamicin (Mylotarg). These medicines are probably in the first generation of treatments that target leukemic cells rather than all dividing cells.

Imatinib mesylate, also called Gleevec, is very effective at producing remission in early-stage CML. Because CML cells produce an abnormal receptor molecule called tyrosine kinase that permanently activates cell division, scientists reasoned that drugs that disable this protein might be able to halt CML. This research strategy was very successful. Gleevec was designed to target the abnormal tyrosine kinase and halt its activity. That is exactly what Gleevec does.

Tretinoin, also sold as Vesanoid, is first-line treatment for APL. This drug is a type of molecule called all-trans retinoic acid (ATRA). ATRA is an important signal molecule used in cell differentiation during normal development. Scientists speculated that leukemic cells are generally "stuck" in an immature, undifferentiated state. They hypothesized that treating APL with differentiating agents, like Vesanoid, would promote the differentiation of immature leukemic cells into more mature functioning ones. The hypothesis was correct: Vesanoid does indeed trigger differentiation of the leukemic cells. Interestingly, if the Vesanoid treatment ceases to be effective, the second line of treatment for APL is arsenic trioxide (Trisenox).

Gemtuzumab ozogamicin, often sold as Mylotarg, is a drug used to treat AML, is yet another focused strategy. In this case, Mylotarg is a specific antibody molecule that recognizes and binds to a particular membrane protein found on AML cells. When Mylotarg binds to the leukemia cells, they are in for a big surprise. Mylotarg is "weaponized," meaning that attached to it is a deadly toxin. As a consequence, Mylotarg can bind specifically to leukemic cells and kill them with its deadly cargo. Because the treatment is so focused, other cells are generally not affected.

Stem Cell Transplantation

In some cases, chemotherapy produces permanent remission. For other patients, remission is stabilized by maintenance chemotherapy, drugs administered at regular intervals for the rest of the patient's life. Unfortunately, leukemic cells sometimes develop resistance to chemotherapy drugs and the cells begin to proliferate once more. Other chemotherapeutic agents will be tried but ultimately, it may be necessary to do a stem cell transplant. In this procedure, the leukemic bone marrow of the patient is destroyed and healthy bone marrow, containing stem cells,

Stem Cell Transplantation

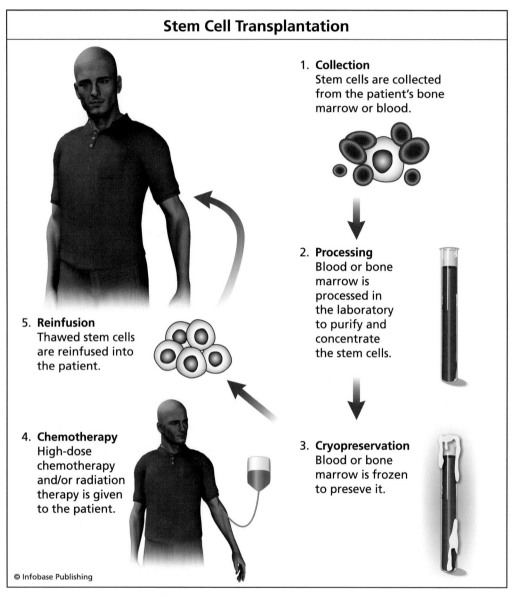

1. **Collection**
   Stem cells are collected from the patient's bone marrow or blood.

2. **Processing**
   Blood or bone marrow is processed in the laboratory to purify and concentrate the stem cells.

3. **Cryopreservation**
   Blood or bone marrow is frozen to preseve it.

4. **Chemotherapy**
   High-dose chemotherapy and/or radiation therapy is given to the patient.

5. **Reinfusion**
   Thawed stem cells are reinfused into the patient.

© Infobase Publishing

Figure 8.1a If chemotherapy has not worked, an autologous stem cell transplantation is the preferred method of destroying leukemic cells and replacing them with healthy cells. The patient is the donor, which means that the body will not reject the transplanted cells.

is collected from a donor and transplanted into the patient. Successful stem cell transplantations actually cure leukemia. These transplantations are not the first choice for treatment, however, because the procedure entails some risks and side effects can be difficult.

Successful transplantations require a good "match" between the donor tissue and recipient tissue. All cell membranes contain a wide variety of embedded proteins. Cells use these proteins for many different functions including cell recognition and communication. In fact, some of these cell membrane proteins allow the body to recognize "self" versus "nonself." All of the cells in a given person have the same types of proteins indicating "self." For this reason, the body's immune system does not attack its own cells. In contrast, tissues or cells transplanted from another body will possess a different set of proteins, which identify themselves as "nonself." As a consequence, the recipient's immune system will kill the transplanted cells. This behavior occurs when the body rejects a transplanted organ.

There are several strategies for getting a good stem cell donor match. The most desired approach is to do an **autologous** transplantation, in which the recipient is also the donor. Physicians collect stem cells from a leukemia patient who is in complete remission. These cells are frozen until they are needed. If the patient relapses, and transplantation is the next appropriate treatment, the physician administers total body irradiation and chemotherapy to kill all cancer cells. After completion of this step, the physician reinfuses the previously frozen stem cells. Because it can take up to two weeks for the first new, healthy leukocytes to occur, the patient remains vulnerable to infections and bleeding during that time.

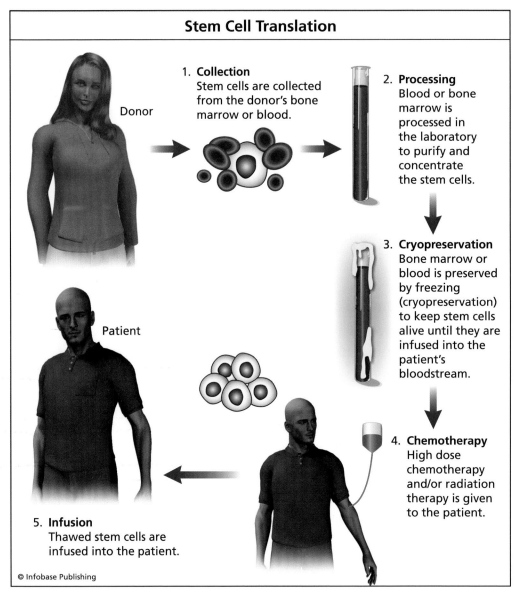

Stem Cell Translation

Donor

1. **Collection**
   Stem cells are collected from the donor's bone marrow or blood.

2. **Processing**
   Blood or bone marrow is processed in the laboratory to purify and concentrate the stem cells.

3. **Cryopreservation**
   Bone marrow or blood is preserved by freezing (cryopreservation) to keep stem cells alive until they are infused into the patient's bloodstream.

Patient

4. **Chemotherapy**
   High dose chemotherapy and/or radiation therapy is given to the patient.

5. **Infusion**
   Thawed stem cells are infused into the patient.

© Infobase Publishing

Figure 8.1b   In an allogenic stem cell transplantation, a donor who is not the patient provides healthy stem cells. Although donors are carefully screened to match the recipient, there is a chance that the patient's body will reject the transplanted cells.

Often, autologous stem cell transplantation is not possible. Instead, **allogeneic** transplantations are performed. The donor is someone other than the recipient. The closer the tissue match between donor and recipient, the greater the chances for success and the fewer side effects. The best allogeneic match is one between identical twins. Next, other blood relatives would be tested. In the absence of a good donor in the patient's family, physicians would next check the National Marrow Donor Program. This organization maintains a searchable record of tissue-typed volunteers so that matches can be found for unrelated donors. Once a donor is located, the physician treats the patient with whole-body radiation and chemotherapy to kill all cancer cells. Next, the stems cells collected from the donor can be transfused into the patient. As is the case with autologous transplantations, it takes a while for normal leukocytes to appear—two to three weeks for an allogeneic transplantation. As a consequence, the patient is at risk for infections and bleeding during this time period. Also, an individual receiving an allogeneic transplantation needs to take additional medicines to suppress his or her immune system's response to "foreign" cells.

There are several sources for stem cells to be used in transplantations. The most usual location for collection is the bone marrow, the tissue where blood-forming cells are found. Stem cells are also harvested directly from the blood. To use this method, stem cells need to be "mobilized," or moved from the bone marrow into the blood. The physician injects the donor with a growth factor for four days. Stem cells are collected daily during this mobilization treatment. The stem cells are frozen for later use. Finally, blood collected from the umbilical cord and placenta contains fetal stem cells. Blood can be recovered from these tissues and frozen for later use.

The principal long-term side effect of stem cell transplantation is **graft-versus-host disease (GVHD)**. Occurring in recipients of allogeneic transplantations, GVHD is a consequence of the immune system's response to

SPOTLIGHT ON CANCER SCIENTISTS:
STEVEN A. ROSENBERG, M.D. PH.D. (1940-)

Steven A. Rosenberg is the Chief of Surgery at the National Cancer Institute (NCI) in Bethesda, Maryland, as well as a Professor of Surgery at the Uniformed Services University of Health Sciences and at the University of Washington School of Medicine and Health Sciences; Dr. Steven Rosenberg has devoted his life to the understanding and treatment of cancer.

Rosenberg earned his bachelor's and medical degrees at Johns Hopkins University. He also received a Ph.D. in biophysics from Harvard University. He became Chief of Surgery at NCI in 1974 and has been there ever since.

Rosenberg has been a pioneer in developing **immunotherapy** for cancer treatment, in which the body's immune system is helped in its fight against cancer cells. He has had some amazing achievements in this area. For example, Rosenberg developed interleukin-2, a natural molecule made by the body, as the first immunotherapy treatment for cancer. He also identified a type of white blood cell that invades tumors and figured out how to use these cells against cancer. Rosenberg and his team have identified more than two dozen types of molecules associated uniquely with cancer cells. Research is under way to see whether it is possible to develop antibodies that will specifically recognize cancer cells and mark them for destruction. Finally, Rosenberg

foreign cells. As the body attacks the offspring of the transplanted cells, symptoms can include skin rashes, dry or irritated eyes, nausea, vomiting, diarrhea, difficulty swallowing, joint stiffness, hardening skin, and liver damage. GVHD can range from mild to life threatening. As one leukemia patient characterized—it is like trading one disease for another.

did the first clinical studies of gene therapy to fight cancer. He took normal white blood cells from 17 patients with malignant melanoma. The white blood cells were modified so that they would recognize the deadly melanoma cells. For two of the patients, the results were spectacular; their cancers were completely eliminated. Before the experiment, these individuals had been told that they would live for no more than another 3 to 6 months. Since the treatment these subjects have been cancer free for years and continue to be checked regularly. As Dr.

Figure 8.2   Dr. Steven Rosenberg. *(National Cancer Institute/U.S. National Institutes of Health)*

Rosenberg says, "This is just a start . . . . [W]e're working around the clock to try to improve this."[4]

FUTURE TREATMENTS

Scientists and physicians continue to engage actively in research aimed at improving therapies for leukemia. Some of the newer treatments that have been developed are already being used for patients. Others are still in the research and development phase.

A new type of stem transplantation that is still in the experimental phase is called **non-ablative allogeneic stem cell transplantation**. With this method, the patient's own stem cells are diminished but not completely knocked out by radiation and chemotherapy. The donor cells are transplanted into the patient and immunosuppressive drugs are used to prevent rejection. The idea is for the donor's cells to establish themselves and produce normal leukocytes that will attack the leukemic cells. Instead of a graft-versus-host attack, scientists predict a "graft-versus-leukemia" effect. The advantage of this new type of transplantation compared to the methods presently used is that the patient can handle it more easily. The standard method, unlike this new one, destroys the patient's immune system and blood cells, a physical event that is very difficult to tolerate.

There are also newer drugs that are either available or in development. For example, Revlimid is used to treat **myelodysplastic syndrome**, a type of blood cell disease. It is effective in the subtypes of leukemia that exhibit an abnormal change in chromosome 5. Also, hairy cell leukemia, a type of CLL, is responsive to the drugs cladribine and pentostatin. In addition, research is under way to develop a **vaccine** against cancer cells.

One of the most successful drug development efforts in recent years produced Gleevec. As already discussed, this drug inhibits the abnormal oncogenic protein produced by *bcr/abl*. The strategy of targeting the products of oncogenes is a powerful one and has also worked for other cancers. For example, the drug trastuzumab (Herceptin) is effective for treating certain types of breast cancers. This drug targets a faulty receptor protein, which is encoded by an oncogene.

Finally, scientists and physicians are also developing treatments that take advantage of some of the self-protective features of the body itself. For example, **hematopoietic** growth factors, molecules that normally function as signals to direct blood cell production and development, can be administered to patients to help them regenerate bone marrow after a bone marrow transplant. Also, **interferons**, molecules normally made by the immune system to fight disease, can be given in higher doses to leukemia patients. The interferons fight the cancer cells and stimulate the body to produce more of its own interferon.

Although techniques for early and accurate diagnosis as well as for effective treatments continue to improve, the best approach for leukemia or any other cancer is to take steps to prevent its occurrence. For leukemia, the known principle risk factors include exposure to high doses of radiation, benzene and certain other chemicals, smoking, and infection with HTLV-1. These factors can generally be avoided quite easily. In most cases, however, leukemia develops with no clear indication of any specific trigger. Because cancer is the result of accumulated genetic errors, everyone bears some chance of developing this disease. If this event occurs, the best action is early detection followed by sensible, aggressive treatment and care.

SUMMARY

A diagnosis of leukemia is based on a physical examination of the patient, an analysis of blood, and a bone marrow biopsy. Physicians examine the blood and bone marrow to see if abnormal leukocytes are present. If such cells are observed, the specific type of leukemia cell is identified and the medical technologist can analyze chromosomes to see if they are normal. The results of these tests are essential for physicians to identify exactly what type of leukemia has occurred and to plan appropriate treatment. Chemotherapy is the main option for all forms of leukemia. In some cases, patients achieve long-term remission. The only certain cure for leukemia is a successful stem cell transplant, but this procedure has its own risks. Scientists are hard at work developing new, more targeted drugs for leukemia as well as improved methods for stem cell transplantation. Although some risk factors for leukemia have been identified and should be avoided when possible, most cases of the disease cannot be attributed to a particular cause or event.

NOTES

♦

Chapter 1

1. The Leukemia and Lymphoma Society. "Leukemia Facts & Statistics." *LLS.org*. Available online. URL: http://leukemia-lymphoma.org. Accessed on March 8, 2007.

2. The Leukemia and Lymphoma Society. "Leukemia Facts & Statistics." *LLS.org*. Available online. URL: http://leukemia-lymphoma.org. Accessed on March 8, 2007.

3. The Leukemia and Lymphoma Society. "Leukemia Facts & Statistics." *LLS.org*. Available online. URL: http://leukemia-lymphoma.org. Accessed on March 8, 2007.

Chapter 2

1. Mel Greaves. *Cancer: The Evolutionary Legacy*. Oxford, England: Oxford University Press, 2001.

2. PBS Nature. "Leech Therapy." *http://www.pbs.org*. Available online. URL: http://www.pbs.org/wnet/nature/bloodysuckers/leech2.html. Accessed August 6, 2008.

3. H. Kuper, H.-O. Adami, and D. Trichopoulos. "Infections as a Major Preventable Cause of Cancer." *Journal of Internal Medicine* 248 (2000): 171–183.

Chapter 3

1. Neil A. Campbell and Jane B. Reece. *Biology*, 7th edition. Menlo Park, California: Benjamin/Cummings, 2004.

2. Brian J. P. Huntly and D. Gary Gilliland. "Leukemia Stem Cells and the Evolution of Cancer-Stem-Cell Research." *Nature Reviews Cancer* 5 (2005): 311–321.

3. Brian J. P. Huntly and D. Gary Gilliland. "Leukemia Stem Cells and the Evolution of Cancer-Stem-Cell Research." *Nature Reviews Cancer* 5 (2005): 311–321.

Chapter 4

1. The Leukemia and Lymphoma Society. "Acute Lymphocytic Leukemia." *LLS.org*. Available online. URL: http://www.leukemia-lymphoma.org. Accessed March 8, 2007.

2. The Leukemia and Lymphoma Society. "Acute Lymphocytic Leukemia." *LLS.org*. Available online. URL: http://www.leukemia-lymphoma.org. Accessed March 8, 2007.

3. Jeffrey E. Rubnitz and Ching-Hon Pui. "Childhood Acute Lymphoblastic Leukemia." *The Oncologist* 2 (1997): 374–380.

4. The Leukemia and Lymphoma Society. "Acute Lymphocytic Leukemia." *LLS.org*. Available online. URL: http://www.leukemia-lymphoma.org. Accessed March 8, 2007.

5. The Leukemia and Lymphoma Society. "Chronic Lymphocytic Leukemia." *LLS.org*. Available online. URL: http://www.leukemia-lymphoma.org. Accessed March 8, 2007.

6. The Leukemia and Lymphoma Society. "Acute Myelogenous Leukemia." *LLS.org*. Available online. URL: http://www.leukemia-lymphoma.org. Accessed March 8, 2007.

7. The Leukemia and Lymphoma Society. "Chronic Myelogenous Leukemia." *LLS.org*. Available online. URL: http://www.leukemia-lymphoma.org. Accessed March 8, 2007.

Chapter 5

1. JLS Foundation. "Children With Leukemia." *Jlsfoundation.org*. Available online. URL: http://jlsfoundation.org/index.htm. Downloaded May 22, 2008.

2. Kids Health for Parents. "Childhood Cancer: Leukemia." *Kidshealth.org*. Available online. URL: http://www.kidshealth.org/parent/medical/cancer/cancer-leukemia.html. Accessed March 8, 2007.

3. Kim Robien and Cornelia M. Ulrich. "5, 10-Methylenetetrahydrofolate Reductase Polymorphisms and Leukemia Risk: A HuGE Minireview." *American Journal of Epidemiology* 157, 7 (2003): 571–582.

4. Jeffrey E. Rubnitz and Ching-Hon Pui. "Childhood Acute Lymphoblastic Leukemia." *The Oncologist* 2 (1997): 374–380.

5. The Leukemia and Lymphoma Society. *LLS.org*. Available online. URL: http://www.leukemia-lymphoma.org. Accessed March 8, 2007.

6. Kids Health for Parents. "Childhood Cancer: Leukemia." *Kidshealth.org*. Available online. URL: http://www.kidshealth.org/parent/medical/cancer/cancer-leukemia.html. Accessed March 8, 2007.

7. C. Gilham, J. Peto, J. Simpson, E. Roman, T.O.B. Eden, M.F. Greaves, F.E. Alexander, for the UKCCS Investigators. "Day Care in Infancy and Risk of Childhood Acute Lymphoblastic Leukaemia: Findings From UK Case-Control Study." *British Medical Journal* 10 (2005): 1–6. Downloaded from bmj.com April 9, 2007.

8. L. Kinlen and R. Doll. "Population Mixing and Childhood Leukaemia: Fallon and Other US Clusters." *British Journal of Cancer* 91 (2004): 1–3.

9. Siobhan M. O'Connor and Roumiana S. Boneva. "Infectious Etiologies of Childhood Leukemia: Plausibility and Challenges to Proof." *Environmental Health Perspectives* 115, no. 1 (2007): 146–150.

10. Michael J. Thun and Thomas Sinks. "Understanding Cancer Clusters." *CA: A Cancer Journal for Clinicians* 54 (2004): 273–280.

11. L. Kinlen, and R. Doll. "Population Mixing and Childhood Leukaemia: Fallon and Other US Clusters." *British Journal of Cancer* 91 (2004): 1–3.

12. Kim Robien and Cornelia M. Ulrich. "5, 10-Methylenetetrahydrofolate Reductase Polymorphisms and Leukemia Risk: A HuGE Minireview." *American Journal of Epidemiology* 157, 7 (2003): 571–582.

13. Dana-Farber Cancer Institute. "Who Was Sidney Farber?" *http://www. dana-farber.org*. Available online. URL: http://www.dana-farber.org/abo/history/who. Accessed August 6, 2008.

14. Medical News Today. "After Treatment for Childhood Leukemia, Rate of Secondary Cancers Increases Over Years." *http://www.medicalnewstoday. com*. Available online. URL: http://www.medicalnewstoday.com/articles/65375.php. Accessed July 18, 2008.

Chapter 6

1. Robert Heyssel, A. Bertrand Brill, Lowell A. Woodbury, Edwin T. Nishimura, Tarunendu Ghose, Takashi Hoshino, and Mitsuru Yamasaki. "Leukemia in Hiroshima Atomic Bomb Survivors." *Blood* 15, 3 (1960): 313–331.

2. Robert D. Lange, William Moloney, and Tokuso Yamawaki. "Leukemia in Atomic Bomb Survivors: I. General Observations." *Blood* 9 (6) (1954): 574–585.

3. Robert Heyssel, A. Bertrand Brill, Lowell A. Woodbury, Edwin T. Nishimura, Tarunendu Ghose, Takashi Hoshino, and Mitsuru Yamasaki. "Leukemia in Hiroshima Atomic Bomb Survivors." *Blood* 15 (3) (1960): 313–331.

4. E.C. Vigliani. "Leukemia Associated With Benzene Exposure." *Annals New York Academy of Sciences* 271 (1976): 143–151.

5. E.C. Vigliani. "Leukemia Associated With Benzene Exposure." *Annals New York Academy of Sciences* 271 (1976): 143–151.

Chapter 7

1. Peter A. Hall. "p53: The Challenge of Linking Basic Science and Patient Management." *The Oncologist* 3 (1998): 218–224.

2. David Malkin. "Germline *p53* Mutations and Heritable Cancer." *Annual Review of Genetics* 28 (1994): 443–465.

3. University of Dundee. "Professor Sir David Lane." *http://www.dundee. ac.uk*. Available online. URL: http://www.dundee.ac.uk/surgery/onestaff2 .php?ID=56. Accessed August 9, 2008.

4. Peter Nowell, Janet Rowley, and Alfred Knudson. "Cancer Genetics, Cyto- genetics—Defining the Enemy Within." *Nature Medicine* 4, no. 10 (1998): 1107–1111.

5. Sandy Smith. "Peter Nowell." *http://www.upenn.edu*. Available online. URL: http://www.upenn.edu/pennnews/current/1999/012899/Nowell. html. Accessed August 9, 2008.

6. Alessandra DiBacco, Karen Keeshan, Sharon L. McKenna, and Thomas G. Cotter. "Molecular Abnormalities in Chronic Myeloid Leukemia: Deregula- tion of Cell Growth and Apoptosis." *The Oncologist* 5 (2005): 405–415.

Chapter 8

1. Cammy Lee Leukemia Foundation Inc. "About Cammy Lee." *Cllf.org*. Available online. URL: http://www.cllf.org/index.php/About-Cammy-Lee. html. Accessed May 22, 2008.

2. Claude E. Forkner and T. F. McNair Scott. "Arsenic as a Therapeutic Agent in Chronic Myelogenous Leukemia." *Journal of the American Medical As- sociation* 97, 1 (1931): 3–5.

3. Claude E. Forkner and T.F. McNair Scott. "Arsenic as a Therapeutic Agent in Chronic Myelogenous Leukemia." *Journal of the American Medical As- sociation* 97, 1 (1931): 3–5.

4. CNNAccess. "Cancer Researcher: 'This is Just a Start.'" *CNN.com*. Available online. URL: http://www.cnn/2006/HEALTH/08/31/cnna.rosenberg/index. html. Accessed August 6, 2008.

GLOSSARY

♦

abscess A localized collection of pus in the body, generally surrounded by inflamed tissue.

accelerated phase In CML, an interval following the chronic phase in which cells accumulate genetic errors and produce more abnormal cells.

acute lymphocytic leukemia (ALL) A fast-growing type of leukemia affecting cells of the lymphoid lineage.

acute myelogenous leukemia (AML) A fast-growing type of leukemia affecting cells of the myeloid lineage.

acute promyelocytic leukemia (APL) A subtype of AML.

allogeneic Transplantation of stem cells from a donor into a host.

anemia; anemic Condition in which there is an inadequate amount of hemoglobin and erythrocytes in the blood.

angiogenesis The growth of new blood vessels.

antibody A protein molecule made by the immune system that can bind to invading. microorganisms, or other foreign material, and disable them.

apoptosis Programmed cell death.

aspiration Removal of bone marrow with a fine needle.

ataxia telangiectasia A genetic disorder associated with immune system problems and loss of muscle coordination.

autologous Transplantation of stored stem cells from a person back into his or her own body.

autopsy Dissection of a cadaver to determine the cause of death and the effects of disease on the body.

basal cell carcinoma A type of skin cancer that is usually not serious and rarely metastasizes.

basophil A type of leukocyte derived from the myeloid lineage.

benign A noncancerous tumor, like a wart, for example.

biopsy Examining a cell or tissue sample to determine if cancer is present.

blast crisis In CML, the most serious stage of the disease, which if untreated will be fatal.

bloodletting Discredited practice of removing blood to "balance" fluids of the body and to remove "bad" materials.

Bloom syndrome An inherited disorder in which chromosomes exhibit a high frequency of breakage.

B lymphocyte A type of leukocyte derived from the lymphoid cell lineage. B-lymphocytes produce antibodies.

bone marrow The spongy material inside bones where blood cells are formed.

cancer The uncontrolled cell proliferation and breakdown of proper cell behavior that results in the development of tumors that can spread throughout the body.

capillary The smallest type of blood vessel in the body.

carcinogen A substance that causes cancer.

carcinoma Cancer of epithelial cells.

catheter A tube inserted into a blood vessel or body cavity.

cervix The neck of the uterus, which connects the uterus to the vagina.

chemotherapy The treatment of cancer with drugs.

chromosomes The structures in cells that carry the genes.

chronic lymphocytic leukemia (CLL) A slowly progressing type of leukemia affecting cells of the lymphoid lineage.

chronic myelogenous leukemia (CML) A slowly progressing type of leukemia affecting cells of the myeloid lineage.

chronic phase In CML, the initial slowly progressing stage of the disease.

clone; clonal Genetically identical cells all originating from one individual cell.

cytogenetics The examination and analysis of the structure of chromosomes in cells.

dendritic cell A type of leukocyte derived from the myeloid lineage. Dendritic cells activate lymphocytes.

dermatologist A physician who specializes in skin and related structures.

differentiation The specialization of cells into specific types of cells.

DNA Deoxyribonucleic acid; the molecule that carries genetic information.

Down syndrome A developmental and physical disorder in which an individual inherits three copies of chromosome number 21 rather than two.

electron microscope A device that focuses an electron beam and magnifies so we can see structures as small as the parts of cells and large molecules.

eosinophils A type of leukocyte derived from the myeloid cell lineage. Eosinophils release chemicals to destroy parasites such as worms.

epithelium, epithelial   Refers to cells organized into a sheet of tissue.

erythema dose   Refers to the amount of radiation required to produce redness of the skin.

erythrocyte   Red blood cells.

Fanconi's anemia   A type of congenital anemia characterized by a deficiency in all types of blood cells.

fluorescence *in situ* hybridization (FISH)   A type of staining method used to analyze chromosome structure.

flow cytometry   A technique that separates a mixed population of cells into its constituent types.

gene   Inherited instructions composed of DNA.

genome   All of the genes in a cell nucleus.

graft-versus-host disease (GVHD)   A potential side effect of allogeneic cell transplantation in which the transplanted cells attack the host cells.

granulocyte   Any type of leukocyte-containing granules.

hematopoesis; hematopoetic   The development and differentiation of blood cells.

hemoglobin   Protein in red blood cells that carries oxygen.

hirudin   Protein in leech saliva that prevents blood clotting.

histamine   Chemicals released by basophils that trigger inflammation.

histology   The study of cells and tissues.

immunization   The process of inducing immunity, often by the injection of a vaccine.

immunophenotype   A technique to determine what type of lymphocyte is abnormal in ALL or CLL.

immunotherapy   Using the body's own immune system as a tool to fight cancer cells.

incidence   The frequency with which an event occurs.

inflammation   A local response to tissue or cellular injury wherein tissues become red, warm, and swollen.

interferon   Molecules produced by the immune system to fight disease.

invasive   Refers to the spread of cancer cells from one part of the body to another.

leukapheresis   A technique used to filter blood to reduce the number of abnormal leukocytes.

leukemia   A type of cancer or malignancy that involves the white blood cells.

leukemic stem cells (LSC)   Self-renewing cells that give rise to leukemia cells.

leukocyte   White blood cell.

Li-Fraumeni syndrome   A genetic disorder that increases the risk of developing several types of cancer.

lumbar puncture   A procedure in which a needle is inserted into the spinal column and spinal fluid is removed.

lymphoid   One of the lineages of the pluripotent stem cells found in the bone marrow, it produces natural killer cells, B lymphocytes, and T lymphocytes.

lymphoma   A type of cancer or malignancy involving the enlargement of the lymph nodes, spleen, and liver.

macrophage   A type of leukocyte that eats bacteria and dirt.

malignant   Cancers that grow uncontrollably and spread to other tissues in the body.

median   The middle of a range of numbers.

medical technologist   A health care professional who performs lab tests and analyses of cells and tissues.

megakaryocyte   Blood cells derived from the myeloid lineage that gives rise to platelets.

melanoma   A highly aggressive, invasive skin cancer.

meningioma   A tumor of the meninges, the covering of the brain and spinal cord.

metastasis   The spread of a cancer from a primary tumor to other places in the body.

monocytes   A type of leukocyte produced by the myeloid cell lineage. Monocytes produce macrophages.

mutation   A change or error in DNA.

myelodysplastic syndrome   A disease characterized by the inadequate production of blood cells.

myeloid   One of the lineages of pluripotent stem cells found in the bone marrow, which produces erythrocytes, megakaryocytes, basophils, eosinophils, neutrophils, monocytes, and dendritic leukocytes.

myeloma   A type of bone marrow cancer.

nasopharynx, nasopharyngeal   Refers to the nose and pharynx, the cavity behind the mouth and nose.

natural killer (NK) cells   A type of leukocyte produced by the lymphoid cell lineage.

neutrophils   A type of leukocyte derived from the myeloid cell lineage. Neutrophils eat invading bacteria.

non-ablative allogeneic stem cell transplantation A technique in which the patient's own stem cells are diminished but not eliminated completely before receiving stem cells from a donor.

nucleus Cell organelle in which chromosomes are located.

Ommaya reservoir A type of catheter inserted under the scalp that can deliver drugs to the brain.

oncogene Cancer-causing gene.

oncogenic Cancer causing.

oncologist A physician who specializes in cancer.

pancreas An organ that secretes digestive enzymes into the small intestine and the hormone insulin into the blood.

pathologist A physician who specializes in the study of disease.

pathology The study of disease.

pernicious anemia A severe anemia caused by the inability to absorb vitamin B12.

phagocytic; phagocytosis A behavior in which cell cells eat other microorganisms or debris.

placenta The organ found in mammals that attaches the embryo or fetus to the uterus, and that delivers oxygen and nutrients to the embryo or fetus.

plasma The liquid portion of blood.

platelets Cell fragments that play an important role in blood clotting.

pluripotent Cells that are not fully differentiated and which can produce various cell types.

prognosis A prediction about the course of a disease.

proliferation Cell division to produce new cells.

proteins Molecules in cells that are essential for cell structure and function.

proto-oncogenes Normal cellular genes that encode molecules regulating cell division, survival, or differentiation. These can be altered to become oncogenes.

psoriasis A skin inflammation condition.

radiation Energy transmitted as waves, rays, or particles.

radiation therapy The treatment of cancer with radiation.

radioactive The emission of radiation from atoms.

receptor A protein that binds to another molecule to initiate some sort of cellular response.

rectum The last section of the large intestine extending from the colon to the anus.

relapse The return of a disease thought to be absent.

remission A decrease or cessation of a disease.

retrovirus A type of virus that has an RNA rather than a DNA genome.

Rous sarcoma virus (**RSV**) An example of a tumorigenic virus.

sarcoma A type of cancer from bone, muscle, or connective tissue.

Schwachman-Diamond syndrome A genetic condition characterized by an improperly functioning pancreas and bone marrow.

scrotum, scrotal Refers to the skin that encloses the testes.

secondary cancers or tumors Cancer that forms at a site other than the original location of a tumor, because of metastasis.

signal molecule A molecule that operates either inside or outside cells to mediate cell communication.

spleen Organ in which lymphocytes form.

stem cells Self-renewing cells that are not differentiated, and that have the ability to make various cell types.

T lymphocyte A type of leukocyte derived from the lymphoid lineage. T-lymphocytes make antibodies.

tissue A group of functionally and structurally similar cells.

topoisomerese II An enzyme essential for DNA repair.

trachea The windpipe; the tube that connects the larynx to the bronchi of the lungs.

transcription factors Proteins that regulate gene activity.

translocation The movement of a piece of chromosome to another chromosomal position.

transformation The changing of a cell from a healthy to a cancerous one.

tropical anemia A type of anemia due to nutritional deficiencies and/or hookworm infestation.

tumor An abnormal mass of cells.

tumor suppressor A substance that stops the growth and development of a tumor.

tyrosine kinase A type of protein involved in cell communication.

vaccine; vaccination Treatment in which weakened or dead disease-causing microorganisms are administered to prevent infection with a specific organism.

virus A parasite much smaller than a cell.

Wilms' tumor A type of kidney cancer that occurs in children.

X-rays A relatively high-energy form of radiation.

BIBLIOGRAPHY

♦

Alberts, Bruce, Dennis Bray, Julian Lewis, Martin Raff, Keith Roberts, and James D. Watson. *Molecular Biology of the Cell*. 3rd ed. New York: Garland, 1994.

Ambrogi, Katherine. "Two Profs Win Prestigious Lasker Research Award." http://www.dailypennsylvanian.com. Available online. URL: http://media.www.dailypennsylvanian.com/media/storage/paper882/news/1998/10/14/Resources/Two-Profs.Win.Prestigious.Lasker.Research.Award-2169504.shtml#cp_article_tools. Accessed August 8, 2008.

American Association of Feline Practitioners and The Cornell Feline Health Center. "Feline Leukemia Virus." *http://www.vet.cornell.edu*. Available online. URL: http://www.vet.cornell.edu/fhc/brochures/felv.html. Accessed May 22, 2008.

American Cancer Society. "A Cancer Treatment in the Spice Cabinet?" *http://www.cancer.org*. Available online. URL: http://www.cancer.org/docroot/NWS/content/NWS_2_1x_A_Cancer_Treatment_in_the_Spi. Accessed August 9, 2008.

———. "The History of Cancer." http://www.cancer.org. Available online. URL: http://www.cancer.org/docroot/CRI/content/CRI_2_6x_the_history_of_cancer_72.asp?sitearea=&level=. Accessed November 18, 2008.

American Society for Microbiology. "American Society for Microbiology Honors Steven A. Rosenberg." *http://www.eukekalert.org*. Available online. URL: http://www.eurekalert.org/pub_releases/2008-07/asfm-asf_6071608.php. Accessed August 6, 2008.

Arnold, Robert. "Environmental Contamination and Cancer Rates." *Journal of Environmental Engineering* August (2002): 669–671.

BBC News. "Gene Therapy Rids Men of Cancer." *News.bbc.co.uk*. Available online. URL: http://news.bbc.co.uk/2/hi/health/5304910.stm. Downloaded August 6, 2008.

Becker, Wayne M., Lewis J. Kleinsmith, and Jeff Hardin. *The World of the Cell*. 6th ed. New York: Pearson-Benjamin Cummings, 2006.

Belson, Martin, Beverely Kingsley, and Adrianne Holmes. "Risk Factors for Acute Leukemia in Children: A Review." *Environmental Health Perspectives* 115 (1): 138–145.

Bennett, John Hughes. "Case of Hypertrophy of the Spleen and Liver, in Which Death Took Place From Suppuration of the Blood." *Edinburgh Medical and Surgical Journal* 64 (1845): 413–422.

Biondi, Andrea, Giuseppe Cimino, Rob Pieters, and Ching-Hon Pui. "Biological and Therapeutic Aspects of Infant Leukemia." *Blood* 96, 1 (2000): 24–33.

Bishop, J. Michael. *How to Win the Nobel Prize*. Cambridge, MA: Harvard University Press, 2003.

Bocchetta, Maurizio and Michele Carbone. "Epidemiology and Molecular Pathology at Crossroads to Establish Causation: Molecular Mechanisms of Malignant Transformation." *Oncogene* 23 (2004): 6484–6491.

Britannica Online Encyclopedia. "Rudolf Virchow." *http://www.britannica.com*. Available online. URL: http://www.britannica.com/EBchecked/topic/629797/Rudolf-Carl-Virchow. Accessed August 6, 2008.

Brittinger, G. "Ernst Neumann." *http://www.ernst-neumann-koenigsberg.de*. Available online. URL: http://www.ernst-neumann-koenigsberg.de/Ernst_Neumann/ernst_neumann.html. Accessed August 9, 2008.

Cairns, John. *Matters of Life and Death: Perspectives on Public Health, Molecular Biology, Cancer, and the Prospects for the Human Race*. Princeton, NJ: Princeton University Press, 1997.

Cammy Lee Leukemia Foundation Inc. "About Cammy Lee." *Cllf.org*. Available online. URL: http://www.cllf.org/index.php/About-Cammy-Lee.html. Accessed May 22, 2008.

Campbell, Neil A. and Jane B. Reece. *Biology*. 7th ed. Menlo Park, Calif.: Benjamin/Cummings, 2004.

Caporaso, Neil, Gerald E. Marti, and Lynn Golden. "Perspectives on Familial Chronic Lymphocytic Leukemia: Genes and the Environment." *Seminars in Hematology* 41, 3 (2004): 201–206.

Cavenee, Webster K., and Raymond L. White. "The Genetic Basis of Cancer." *Scientific American* 272, 3 (1995): 72–79.

Charames, George S. and Bharati Bapat. "Genomic Instability and Cancer." *Current Molecular Medicine* 3 (2003): 589–596.

CNNAccess. "Cancer Researcher: 'This is Just a Start.'" *CNN.com*. Available online. URL: http://www.cnn/2006/HEALTH/08/31/cnna.rosenberg/index.html. Accessed August 6, 2008.

Cooper, Geoffrey M. *The Cell: A Molecular Approach*. 2nd ed. Washington, D.C.: ASM Press, 2000.

Craigie, David. "Case of the Spleen, in Which Death Took Place From the Presence of purulent matter in the blood." *Edinburgh Medical and Surgical Journal* 64 (1845): 400–413.

Dahring, Wendy. "Rudolf Ludwig Karl Virchow." *EMuseum@Minnesota State University, Mankato.* Available online. URL: http://www.mnsu.edu/emuseum/information/biography/uvwxyz/virchow_rudolf.html. Accessed August 6, 2008.

Dana-Farber Cancer Institute. "Who was Sidney Farber?" *http://www.dana-farber.org*. Available online. URL: http://www.dana-farber.org/abo/history/who. Accessed August 6, 2008.

Debernardi, Silvana, Debra Lillington, and Bryan Young. "Understanding Cancer at the Chromosome Level: 40 Years of Progress." *European Journal of Cancer* 40 (2004): 1960–1967.

DiBacco, Alessandra, Karen Keeshan, Sharon L. McKenna, and Thomas G. Cotter. "Molecular Abnormalities in Chronic Myeloid Leukemia: Deregulation of Cell Growth and Apoptosis." *The Oncologist* 5 (2005): 405–415.

DiGiovanni, Jackie. "Rudolf Virchow- Founder of Modern Pathology." *Suite101.com*. Available online. URL: http://suite101.com/article.cfm/biographies_scientists/95171. Accessed August 6, 2008.

Diamanopoulos, George T. "Cancer: An Historical Perspective." *Anticancer Research* 16 (1996): 1595–1602.

Dockerty, John D., J. Mark Elwood, David C. G. Skegg, and G. Peter Herbison. "Electromagnetic Field Exposures and Childhood Leukaemias in New Zealand." *The Lancet* 345 (1999): 1967–1968.

Drugstore Museum. "Fowler's Solution, Liquor Arsenicalis, Liquor Potass.E Arsentitis." *drugstoremuseum.com*. Available online. URL:

http:// drugstoremuseum.com/sections/level_info2.php?level_ id=145d%22vel =2%20. Accessed August 9, 2008.

Duvoix, A., F. Morceau, M. Schnekenburger, S. Delhalle, M. M. Galteau, M. Dicato, and M. Diederich. "Curcumin-Induced Cell Death in Two Leukemia Cell Lines: K562 and Jurkat." *Annals of the New York Academy of Sciences* 1010 (2003): 389–392.

Emerson, Ole Daniel. "Giovanni Battista Morgagni." *Who Named It?* Available online. URL: http://whonamedit.com/doctor.cfm/312/html. Accessed August 6, 2008.

Ewald, Paul W. *Plague Time: The New Germ Theory of Disease*. New York: Anchor Books, 2002.

Fidler, Isaiah J. "The Pathogenesis of Cancer Metastasis: The Seed and Soil Hypothesis Revisited." *Nature Reviews Cancer* 3 (2003): 1–6.

Forkner, Claude E. and T. F. McNair Scott. "Arsenic as a Therapeutic Agent in Chronic Myelogenous Leukemia." *Journal of the American Medical Association* 97, no. 1 (1931): 3–5.

Friedberg, Errol C. "How Nucleotide Excision Repair Protects Against Cancer." *Nature Reviews Cancer* 1 (2001): 22–33.

Gallucci, Betty B. "Selected Concepts of Cancer as a Disease: From the Greeks to 1900." *Oncology Nursing Forum* 12, 4 (1985): 67–71.

Gibbs, W. Wayt. "Untangling the Roots of Cancer." *Scientific American* 289, 1 (2003): 56–65.

Gilham, C., J. Peto, J. Simpson, E. Roman, T. O. B. Eden, M. F. Greaves, F. E. Alexander, for the UKCCS Investigators. "Day Care in Infancy and Risk of Childhood Acute Lymphoblastic Leukaemia: Findings From UK Case–Control Study." *British Medical Journal* 10 (2005): 1–6. Available online. URL: http://www.bmj.com. Accessed April 9, 2007.

Graf, J. "Medical Use of Medicinal Leeches." *http://www.uconn.edu*. Available online. URL: http://web.uconn.edu/mcbstaff/graf/AvHm/MedUsemain. htm. Accessed August 6, 2008.

Greaves, Mel. *Cancer: The Evolutionary Legacy*. Oxford, England: Oxford University Press, 2001.

———. "Molecular Genetics, Natural History and the Demise of Childhood Leukaemia." *European Journal of Cancer* 35, no. 2 (1999): 173–185.

Greaves, Mel F., Ana Teresa Maia, Joseph L. Wiemels, and Anthony M. Ford. "Leukemia in Twins: Lessons in Natural History." *Blood* 102, no. 7 (2003): 2321–2333.

Greaves, Mel F., S. M. Colman, M. E. J. Beard, K. Bradstock, M. E. Cabrera, P.-M. Chen, P. Jacobs, P. R. L. Lam-Po-Tang, L. G. MacDougall, C. K. O. Williams, and F. E. Alexander. "Geographical Distribution of Acute Lymphoblastic Leukaemia Subtypes: Second Report of the Collaborative Group Study." *Leukemia* 7, no. 1 (1993): 27–34.

Hahn, William C., and Robert A. Weinberg. "Rules for Making Human Tumor Cells." *New England Journal of Medicine* 347, 20 (2002): 1593–1603.

Hall, Peter A. "p53: The Challenge of Linking Basic Science and Patient Management." *The Oncologist* 3 (1998): 218–224.

Harris, Henry. "Putting on the Brakes." *Nature* 427 (2004): 201.

Heyssel, Robert, A. Bertrand Brill, Lowell A. Woodbury, Edwin T. Nishimura, Tarunendu Ghose, Takashi Hoshino, and Mitsuru Yamasaki. "Leukemia in Hiroshima Atomic Bomb Survivors." *Blood* 15, 3 (1960): 313–331.

Hood, Ernie. "Passing Along Pesticides: Lymphoma Rises in Children of Applicators." *Environmental Health Perspectives* 112, 5 (2004): A300.

Huntly, Brian J. P. and D. Gary Gilliland. "Leukemia stem cells and the evolution of cancer-stem-cell research." *Nature Reviews Cancer* 5 (2005): 311–321.

JLS Foundation. "Children With Leukemia." *Jlsfoundation.org.* Available online. URL: http://jlsfoundation.org/index.htm. Accessed May 22, 2008.

Kardinal, Carl G., and John W. Yarbro. "A Conceptual History of Cancer." *Seminars in Oncology* 6, no. 4 (1979): 396–407.

Kasten, Frederick H. "Paul Ehrlich: Pathfinder in Cell Biology. 1. Chronicle of His Life and Accomplishments in Immunology, Cancer Research, and Chemotherapy." *Biotechnic & Histochemistry* 71, 1 (1996): 2–37.

Kids Health for Parents. "Childhood Cancer: Leukemia." *Kidshealth.org.* Available online. URL: http://kidshealth.org/parent/medical/cancer/cancer_leukemia.html. Accessed November 18, 2008.

Kinlen, L. and R. Doll. "Population Mixing and Childhood Leukaemia: Fallon and Other US Clusters." *British Journal of Cancer* 91 (2004): 1–3.

Koretsky, Gary A. "The Legacy of the Philadelphia Chromosome." *The Journal of Clinical Investigation* 117, no. 8 (2007): 2030–2032.

Kuper, H., H.-O. Adami and D. Trichopoulos. "Infections As a Major Preventable Cause of Cancer." *Journal of Internal Medicine* 248 (2000): 171–183.

Kurzrock, Razelle, Hagop M. Kantarjian, Brian J. Druker, and Moshe Talpaz. "Philadelphia Chromosome—Positive Leukemias: From Basic Mechanisms to Molecular Therapeutics." *Annals of Internal Medicine* 138 (2003): 819–830.

Lai, P. K. and J. Roy. "Antimicrobial and Chemopreventative Properties of Herbs and Spices." *Current Medicinal Chemistry* 11 (2004): 1451–1460.

Lange, Robert D., William Moloney, and Tokuso Yamawaki. "Leukemia in Atomic Bomb Survivors: I. General Observations." *Blood* 9, 6 (1954): 574–585.

Lasker Foundation. "Albert Lasker Clinical Research Award." http://www.laskerfoundation.org. Available online. URL: http://www.laskerfoundation.org/awards/1998_c_presentation.htm. Accessed November 18, 2008.

Latonen, Leena and Marikki Laiho. "Cellular UV Damage Responses—Function of Tumor Suppressor p53." *Biochimica et Biophysica Acta* 1755 (2005): 71–89.

Lee, Ki Won, Hyong Joo Lee, and Chang Yong Lee. "Vitamins, Phytochemicals, Diets, and Their Implementation in Cancer Prevention." *Critical Reviews in Food Science and Nutrition* 44 (2004): 437–452.

Leiss, Jack K. and David A. Savitz. "Home Pesticide Use and Childhood Cancer: A Case–Control Study." *American Journal of Public Health* 85, no. 2 (1995): 249–252.

Leukemia and Lymphoma Society. "Acute Lymphocytic Leukemia." *LLS. org*. Available online. URL: http://www.leukemia-lymphoma.org/all_page?item_id=7049. Accessed November 18, 2008.

————. "Chronic Lymphocytic Leukemia." *LLS.org*. Available online. URL: http://www.leukemia-lymphoma.org/all_page?item_id=7059. Accessed November 18, 2008.

————. "Acute Myelogenous Leukemia." *LLS.org*. Available online. URL: http://www.leukemia-lymphoma.org/all_page?item_id=8459. Accessed November 18, 2008.

————. "Chronic Myelogenous Leukemia." *LLS.org*. Available online. URL: http://www.leukemia-lymphoma.org/all_page?item_id=8501. Accessed November 18, 2008.

————. "Hairy Cell Leukemia." *LLS.org*. Available online. URL: http://www.leukemia-lymphoma.org/all_page?item_id=8507. Accessed November 18, 2008.

————. "Leukemia." *LLS.org*. Available online. URL: http://www.leukemia-lymphoma.org/all_page?item_id=7026. Accessed November 18, 2008.

————. "Leukemia Facts & Statistics." *LLS.org*. Available online. URL: http://www.leukemia-lymphoma.org/all_page?item_id=12486. Accessed November 18, 2008.

Lewis, Carol. "Living With Leukemia." http://www.fda.org. Available online. URL: http://www.fda.gov/Fdac/features/2002/202_leuk.html. Accessed May 22, 2008.

Li, Frederick P. and Joseph F. Fraumeni. "Soft-Tissue Sarcomas, Breast Cancer, and Other Neoplasms: A Familial Syndrome?" *Annals of Internal Medicine* 71, 4 (1969): 747–752.

Lodish, Harvey, Arnold Berk, Paul Matsudaira, Chris A. Kaiser, Monty Krieger, Matthew P. Scott, S. Lawrence Zipursky, and James Darnell. *Molecular Cell Biology*. 5th ed. New York: W. H. Freeman, 2004.

Malkin, David. "Germline *p53* Mutations and Heritable Cancer." *Annual Review of Genetics* 28 (1994): 443–465.

Mayo Clinic Staff. "Curcumin: Can It Slow Cancer Growth?" *MayoClinic.com*. Available online. URL: http://www.mayoclinic.com/print/curcumin/AN0174/METHOD=print. Accessed August 9, 2008.

McGrayne, Sharon Bertsch. *Nobel Prize Women in Science*. 2nd ed. Secaucus, NJ: Citadel Press Books, 1998.

McKinnell, Robert G., Ralph E. Parchment, Alan O. Perantoni, Ivan Damjanov, and G. Barry Pierce. *The Biological Basis of Cancer*, 2nd ed. New York: Cambridge University Press, 2006.

Medical News Today. "After Treatment for Childhood Leukemia, Rate of Secondary Cancers Increases Over Years." http://www.medicalnewstoday.com. Available online. URL: http://www.medicalnewstoday.com/articles/65375.php. Downloaded July 18, 2008.

———. "How Curcumin Helps Fight Cancer." http://www.medicalnewstoday.com. Available online. URL: http://www.medicalnewstoday.com/printerfriendlynews.php?newsid=72129. Accessed November 18, 2008.

Mercat-Rommens, Catherine, Didier Louvat, Celine Duffa, and Anne Sugier. "Comparison Between Radiological and Chemical Health Risks Assessments: The Nord-Cotentin Study." *Human and Ecological Risk Assessment* 11 (2005): 627–644.

National Cancer Institute. "Childhood Acute Myeloid Leukemia/Other Malignancies Treatment." http://www.cancer.gov. Available online. URL: http://www.cancer.gov/cancertopics/pdq/treatment/child/AML/patient/allpages/print. Accessed November 18, 2008.

———. "Childhood Lymphoblastic Leukemia Treatment." http://www.cancer.gov. Available online. URL: http://www.cancer.gov/cancertopics/pdq/treatment/childALL/patient/allpages/print. Accessed July 18, 2008.

———. "Steven A. Rosenberg, M.D., Ph.D." http://www.cancer.gov. Available online. URL: http://ccr.cancer.gov/staff/staff.asp?profileid=5757. Accessed August 6, 2008.

———. "What You Need to Know About Leukemia." http://www.cancer.gov. Available online. URL: http://www.cancer.gov/cancertopics/wyntk/leukemia/allpages/print. Accessed November 18, 2008.

Nobel Foundation. "Johannes Fibiger." *Nobelprize.org*. Available online. URL: http://nobelprize.org/nobel_prizes/medicine/laureates/1926/fibiger-bio.html. Accessed November 18, 2008.

———. "Paul Ehrlich." Nobelprize.org. Available online. URL: http://nobelprize.org/nobel_prizes/medicine/laureates/1908/ehrlich-bio.html. Accessed November 18, 2008.

Nowell, Peter, Janet Rowley, and Alfred Knudson. "Cancer Genetics, Cyto-genetics—Defining the Enemy Within." *Nature Medicine* 4, 10 (1998): 1107–1111.

"Obituary. John Hughes Bennett, M.D., F.R.S.E." *The British Medical Journal* October 9 (1875): 473–478.

O'Connor, Siobhan M. and Roumiana S. Boneva. "Infectious Etiologies of Childhood Leukemia: Plausibility and Challenges to Proof." *Environmental Health Perspectives* 115, 1 (2007): 146–150.

Oliff, Allen, Jackson B. Gibbs, and Frank McCormick. "New Molecular Targets for Cancer Therapy." *Scientific American* 275, 3 (1996): 144–149.

Online Mendelian Inheritance in Man. "Li-Fraumeni Syndrome; LFS1." *Nih.gov.* Available online. URL: http://www.ncbi.nlm.nih.gov/entrez/query.fcgi?cmd=Retreive&db=OMIM. Accessed September 13, 2005.

Patlak, Margie. "Targeting Leukemia: From Bench to Bedside." http://www.faseb.org. Available online. URL: http://opa.faseb.org/pdf/leukemia.pdf. Accessed November 18, 2008.

PBS Nature. "Leech Therapy." http://www.pbs.org. Available online. URL: http://www.pbs.org/wnet/nature/bloodysuckers/leech2.html. Accessed August 6, 2008.

Peto, Julian. "Cancer Epidemiology in the Last Century and the Next Decade." *Nature* 444 (2001): 390–395.

Pickrell, John. "Cancer Causer?" *Science News* 162, 11 (2002): 179–180.

Rennie, John, and Ricki Rusting. "Making Headway against Cancer." *Scientific American* 275, 3 (1996): 56–59.

Richardson, David B., Steve Wing, Jane Schroeder, Inga Schmitz-Feuerhake, and Wolfgang Hoffmann. "Ionizing Radiation and Chronic Lymphocytic Leukemia." *Environmental Health Perspectives* 113, 1 (2005): 1–5.

Robien, Kim and Cornelia M. Ulrich. "5, 10-Methylenetetrahydrofolate Reductase Polymorphisms and Leukemia Risk: A HuGE Minireview." *American Journal of Epidemiology* 157, 7 (2003): 571–582.

Rubnitz, Jeffrey E., and Ching-Hon Pui. "Childhood Acute Lymphoblastic Leukemia." *The Oncologist* 2 (1997): 374–380.

Seigworth, Gilbert R. "Bloodletting Over the Centuries." http://www.pbs. org. Available online. URL: http://www.pbs.org/wnet/redgold/basics/ bloodlettinghistory.html. Accessed August 6, 2008.

Sherbenou, Daniel W. and Brian J. Druker. "Applying the Discovery of the Philadelphia Chromosome." *The Journal of Clinical Investigation* 117, 8 (2007): 2067–2074.

Sidransky, David. "Advances in Cancer Detection." *Scientific American* 275, 3 (1996): 104–109.

Sieber, Oliver M., Karl Heinmann, and Ian P. M. Tomlinson. "Genomic Instability—The Engine of Tumorigenesis?" *Nature Reviews Cancer* 3 (2003): 701–708.

Smith, Roger. "Arsenic: A Murderous History." *Dartmouth Toxic Metals Research Program*. Available online. URL: http://www.dartmouth. edu/~toxmetal/TXSHas.shtml. Accessed August 9, 2008.

Smith, Sandy. "Peter Nowell." http://www.upenn.edu. Available online. URL: http://www.upenn.edu/pennnews/current/1999/012899/Nowell.html. Accessed August 9, 2006.

Sohn, Emily. "Targeted Attack: Scientists Declare War on a Protein Implicated in Some Stubborn Forms of Cancer." *Science News* 168 (2005): 139–140.

Starr, Douglas. "Red Gold: The Epic Story of Blood. Early Practices." http:// www.pbs.org. Available online. URL: http://www.pbs.org/wnet/red-gold/basics/bloodletting.html. Accessed August 6, 2008.

St. Jude's Children's Research Hospital. "Hormone Helps Childhood Leukemia Patients Regain Normal Height." http://www.stjude.org. Available online. URL: http://www.stjude.org/media/0,2561,453-2148-3216,00. html. Accessed May 21, 2007.

Strax, Jacqueline. "Turmeric." http://www.psa-rising.com. Available online. URL: http://www.psa-rising.com/eatingwell/turmeric.htm. Accessed August 9, 2008.

Thun, Michael J., and Thomas Sinks. "Understanding Cancer Clusters." *CA: A Cancer Journal for Clinicians* 54 (2004): 273–280.

Trichopoulos, Dimitrios, Frederick P. Li, and David J. Hunter. "What Causes Cancer?" *Scientific American* 275, 3 (1996): 80–87.

University of Dundee. "Professor Sir David Lane." http://www.dundee.ac.uk. Available online. URL: http://www.dundee.ac.uk/surgery/onestaff2 .php?ID=56. Accessed August 9, 2008.

U.S. Department of Energy Office of History and Heritage Resources. "The Manhattan Project." *http://www.cfo.doe.gov.* Available online. URL: http://www.cfo.doe.gov/me70/manhattan/war_1945.htm. Accessed July 18, 2008.

U.S. Food and Drug Administration. "Beyond Bloodletting: FDA Gives Leeches a Medical Makeover." *http://www.fda.gov.* Available online. URL: http://www.fda.gov/fdac/features/2004/504_leech.html. Accessed August 6, 2008.

————. "The New Drug Approval Process." *http://www.fda.gov.* Available online. http://www.fda.gov/cder/handbook/develop.htm. Accessed November 18, 2008.

Vigliani, E. C. "Leukemia Associated With Benzene Exposure." *Annals New York Academy of Sciences* 271 (1976): 143–151.

Walsh, J. J. "Giovanni Battista Morgagni." *The Catholic Encyclopedia.* Available online. URL: http://www.newadvent.org/cathen/10567c.htm. Accessed August 6, 2008.

Waxman, Samuel and Kenneth C. Anderson. "History of the Development of Arsenic Derivatives in Cancer Therapy." *The Oncologist* 6 (2001): 3–10.

Weinberg, Robert A. "How Cancer Arises." *Scientific American* 275, 3 (1996): 62–70.

Willett, Walter C., Graham A. Colditz, and Nancy E. Mueller. "Strategies for Minimizing Risk." *Scientific American* 275, 3 (1996): 88–95.

Zahm, Shelia Hoar and Susan S. Devesa. "Childhood Cancer: Overview of Incidence Trends and Environmental Carcinogens." *Environmental Health Perspectives Supplements* 103, 6 (1995): 177–184.

Zhang, Ting-Dong, Guo-Qiang Chen, Zhu-Gang Wang, Zhen-Yi Wang, Sai-Juan Chen, and Zhu Chen. "Arsenic Trioxide, a Therapeutic Agent for APL." *Oncogene* 20 (2001): 7146–7153.

FURTHER RESOURCES

♦

Books and Articles

Abramovitz, Melissa. *Leukemia.* San Diego, California: Lucent Books, 2002.

Benowitz, Steven I. *Cancer.* Berkeley Heights, NJ: Enslow, 1999.

Bishop, J. Michael. *How to Win the Nobel Prize*. Cambridge, Mass.: Harvard University Press, 2003.

Bozzone, Donna M. *Cancer Genetics.* New York: Chelsea House, 2007.

———. *Causes of Cancer.* New York: Chelsea House, 2007.

Cairns, John. *Matters of Life and Death: Perspectives on Public Health, Molecular Biology, Cancer, and the Prospects for the Human Race.* Princeton, NJ: Princeton University Press, 1997.

Greaves, Mel. *Cancer: The Evolutionary Legacy.* Oxford, England: Oxford University Press, 2003.

Lyons, Lyman. *Diagnosis and Treatment of Cancer.* New York: Chelsea House, 2007.

"What You Need to Know About Cancer," Special Issue, *Scientific American* 275, 3 (1996): 56–167.

Varmus, Harold E. and Robert A Weinberg. *Genes and Cancer.* New York: Scientific American Library, 1993.

Yount, Lisa. *Cancer.* Belmont, Calif., Thomson Gale, 2000.

Web Sites

American Cancer Society (ACS)
http://www.cancer.org/docroot/home/index.asp

Cancerbackup—Europe's leading cancer information service
http://www.cancerbacup.org.uk/Home

Centers for Disease Control (CDC)
http://www.cdc.gov

Leukemia and Lymphoma Society
http://www.LLS.org/hm_lls

National Cancer Institute
http://www.cancer.gov
http://www.nci.nih.gov/cancertopics

INDEX

♦

A

abl gene. *See* genes, *abl* gene
abscess, 55
accelerated phase, 65
actinomycin D, 83
acute lymphocytic leukemia (ALL). *See*
   also childhood leukemia; leukemia
      causes of, 58, 64
      common in children, 58, 74, 75,
         78–79, 83
      described, 12, 58, 59
      treatment, 85–87, 117
      type of leukemia, 54, 56, 70
acute myelogenous leukemia (AML). *See*
   also leukemia
      age of onset, 62
      causes of, 64
      common in children, 62, 72, 74, 81
      described, 62–64
      diagnosis, 62
      risk factors, 64
      subtypes, 62, 122
      treatment, 62, 125
      type of leukemia, 54, 57, 70
acute promyelocytic leukemia (APL), 63,
   122, 123, 125
adult T-cell leukemia, 88, 99–100, 101
age and cancer. *See* cancer, age and;
   leukemia, age of onset
ALL. *See* acute lymphocytic leukemia
allogenic stem cell transportation, 128,
   129
all-trans retinoic acid (ATRA), 63, 125
aminopterin, 83
AML. *See* acute myelogenous leukemia
anemic condition, 17
angiogenesis, 80
antibodies, 47
APL. *See* acute promyelocytic leukemia
apoptosis, 63, 65
appendicitis, 30–31, 50
arsenic, 123
arsenic trioxide therapy, 122–123
asbestos fibers, 34
aspiration, 120

ataxia telangiectasia, 103
ATRA. *See* all-trans retinoic acid
Australopithecus, 6
autologous stem cell transportation, 126,
   127
autopsy, 18, 31
Ayurvedic medicine, 80

B

Baltimore, David, 99
Bang, Oluf, 97
basal cell carcinoma, 86
basophil, 41, 48
bcr/abl gene. *See* genes, *bcr/abl* gene
bcr gene. *See* genes, *bcr* gene
benign tumor, 14
Bennett, John Hughes, 18–19, 37
benzene, 64, 88, 94–95, 96, 101, 104, 133
biopsy, 77. *See also* bone marrow,
   biopsy
Bittner, John, 98
Bittner virus, 98
blast crisis, 65–66
blood
      cancer of. *See* leukemia
      cell counts, 118–119
      cell development and function,
         38–53
      described, 20–21
      proliferation of — cells, 22
"blood drives," 21
bloodletting, 19, 27, 28
Bloom syndrome, 103
B lymphocytes, 43
bone marrow
      biopsy, 61, 116, 133
      blood cell formation/development,
         41, 43, 52, 56–57
      defined, 12–13
      sample, 119–120
      stem cell source, 129
      transplant, 72–73
Borgomano, C., 94
Boston City Hospital, 122
Boveri, Theodor, 110

brain tumor, 86
breakpoint cluster region. *See bcr* gene
breast cancer, 25
Burkitt's lymphoma, 6, 24

C

Cammy Lee Leukemia Foundation
 (CLLF), 118
Campbell, Peter, 54–55
cancer
 age and, 7, 54
 causes of, 34–35
 cytogenetics, 112
 defined, 12
 history of, 6–7, 24–33
 life expectancy, 7
 overview of, 13–15
 patterns of, 34–35
 secondary cancer, 64, 71, 86, 87
 treatment. *See* treatment
"cancer cluster," 79
capillaries, 33
carcinogen, 34
carcinoma, 25, 86
"Case of Hypertrophy of the Spleen and
 Liver" (Bennett), 18
catheter, 124
cats and leukemia, 100
cells
 theory, 27, 32–33
 types of, 13
*Cellular Pathology as Based Upon
Physiological and Pathological Histology*
(Virchow), 33
cervix, cancer of, 25
chemicals, exposure to, 23, 34, 61, 81, 84,
 88, 94–97, 101, 104, 133
chemotherapy
 "collateral damage" from, 64, 104
 defined, 12
 field of, 45
 side effects, 72, 116, 124
 as treatment, 61, 72, 81, 85, 97, 116,
 120, 121–125, 132, 134
Chernobyl nuclear accident, 84
chicken leukemia, 9
childhood leukemia. *See also* acute
lymphocytic leukemia; acute myelogenous leukemia
 causes of, 71, 77–81, 84
 described, 72–73

diagnosis, 76–77
gender incidences, 74
risk factor, 77–78, 81, 84
symptoms of, 71, 74, 76, 87
treatment, 71, 84–87
in twins, 76
types of, 74–76, 132
Children's Hospital (Boston, MA), 82
chromosomes
 changes in, 102–115
 chromosome 9, 67–68
 chromosome 22, 67–68, 113, 114
 described, 16
 Philadelphia chromosome, 54, 67,
 69, 102, 109–114, 115, 117
chronic lymphocytic leukemia (CLL).
 See also leukemia
 age of onset, 58–59
 blood sample from, 36
 causes of, 60, 64
 described, 58–61
 diagnosis, 59
 family patterns, 61
 race and —, 60–61
 risk factors, 60, 61
 survival rates, 61
 treatment, 61
 type of leukemia, 54, 56, 70
chronic myelogenous leukemia (CML).
 See also leukemia
 age of onset, 64
 cell damage in, 110–113, 115
 in children, 74
 common in atomic bomb survivors,
 91
 described, 64–70
 phases of, 64–66
 risk factors, 69
 treatment, 122, 124
 type of leukemia, 54, 57, 70
chronic phase, 64
circulatory system problems, 123
cladribine, 132
clinical trials, 66
CLLF. *See* Cammy Lee Leukemia
 Foundation
clone, 52
Cohnheim, Julius, 48, 52
connective tissues, 27
consolidation therapy, 85
contamination, radiation, 90
A Counterblaste to Tobacco (James I), 34

Craigie, David, 18, 37
curcumin, 80
Curie, Irene, 92–93
Curie, Marie, 92–93
Curie, Pierre, 92
cytogenetics, 18

D

Delore, P., 94
dendritic cells, 43
deoxyribonucleic acid. *See* DNA
dermatologist, 123
diagnosis of leukemia, 17–19, 57, 76–77,
    118–120
Dick, John, 52
diet, 8, 81, 104
differentiation of cell types, 13
differentiation therapy, 62–63
digestive system distress, 123
disease and leukemia risk, 103–104
DNA
        defects in, 7, 8, 103–108, 109, 110
        flow of genetic information, 13, 16
Down syndrome, 84, 103–104
drug. *See also specific drugs*
        development, 66, 70
        immunosuppressive, 84

E

Egypt, 6, 24–25, 28, 37, 121
Ehrlich, Paul, 44–45
electrical power plants, 84
electron microscope, 99
Ellerman, Vilhelm, 97
"embryonic-like" cell, 50
Enola Gay, 89
eosinophil, 41, 47–48
erythema dose, 121
erythrocyte, 38–41, 46, 48, 52–53, 57
exercise, 8, 43
external beam radiation, 121

F

Fallon, Nevada, 79
fallout, radiation, 90
Fanconi's anemia, 84
Farber, Sidney A., 82–83
fatigue, side effect of treatment, 85, 116
FDA. *See* Food and Drug Administration
feline leukemia, 100

FeLV, 100
fertility issues, 124
Fialkow, Philip, 52
Fibiger, Johannes, 98–99
Fidler, Isaiah, 69
"fire drill," 25
FISH. *See* fluorescence *in situ* hybridiza-
    tion
flow cytometry, 119
fluorescence *in situ* hybridization
    (FISH), 119
folate consumption, 81
Food and Drug Administration (FDA),
    29, 66, 123
Fowler's solution, 122, 123
Frieben, Albert, 90

G

Galen, 25, 26
gemtuzumab ozogamicin. *See* Mylotarg
gender incidences, 21–22, 74
genes
        abl gene, 68, 114
        bcr/abl gene, 68, 114, 132
        bcr gene, 114
        categories of, 13
        changes in, 102–115
genetics and leukemia, 61, 102–115
genome, 101
Gleevec (imatinib), 70, 114, 124, 132–133
graft-versus-host disease, 116, 130–131,
    132
graft-versus-leukemia effect, 132
granulocyte lineage, 62
Greeks, 20, 25, 27, 37
Gross, Ludwik, 98
growth hormone production, 85

H

hair loss, 85, 116, 1236, 124
hairy cell leukemia, 132
Hanseman, David von, 109
Hart, Ian, 69
Harvard Medical School, 82
Harvard University, 130
heart problems, 123
hematology, 56
hematopoiesis, 41, 42, 43
hematopoietic growth factors, 133
hemoglobin, 43

herbicides, 61, 88, 95, 97
Herceptin (trastuzumab), 8, 133
Hill, John, 34
Hippocrates, 25, 27
Hiroshima, Japan, 88–91
hirudin, 28
Hirudo medicinalis, 29. *See also* leeches
histamines, 48
histology, 19
Homo erectus, 6
HTLV-1. *See* human thymus-derived
    T-cell leukemia virus
human thymus-derived T-cell leukemia
    virus (HTLV-1), 88, 99–100, 101, 104,
    133
Hungerford, David, 67, 110–111, 113

I

imatinib. *See* Gleevec
immunization, 45
immunophenotyping technique, 58
immunotherapy, 130
Incas, 24
incidence rates, 21
India, 25, 28, 37, 80
induction therapy, 85
infant leukemia, 71, 74
infection, cause of leukemia, 97–101
inflammation, 48
INK4. See tumor suppressor gene
Innocent VII (pope), 21
intensification therapy, 85
interferons, 133

J

James I (king), 34

K

Keller, Kathy, 11–12
Keller, Neil, 11–13
Kochanowicz, Tom, 38–39

L

lancing, 27
Lane, David, 109
Leakey, Louis, 6, 24
Lee, Cammy, 117–118
leeches, 27, 28–29, 55
leukapheresis, 72

leukemia. *See also* acute lymphocytic
leukemia; acute myelogenous leukemia;
childhood leukemia; chronic lymphocytic leukemia; chronic myelogenous
leukemia
    age of onset, 54, 57, 58–59, 62, 64
    blood cells and —, 43–48
    cancer of the blood, 15–19
    causes of, 58, 60, 64, 77–81, 84,
        88–101
    chromosomes changes. *See*
        chromosomes, changes in
    defined, 12
    described, 11–22
    diagnosis of. *See* diagnosis of
        leukemia
    gene changes. *See* genes, changes
        in
    gender issues. *See* gender inci-
        dences
    history of, 35–37
    rates of. *See* incidence rates
    risk factors, 60, 61, 64, 69, 79–81, 84,
        88–101, 102–115, 133
    survival rates. *See* survival rates
    symptoms. *See* symptoms, of
        leukemia
    treatment. *See* treatment
    types of, 54–70. *See also specific
        types of leukemia*
leukemic stem cell (LSC), 48–52, 53
leukocytes, 38–41, 45–46, 48, 49, 52–53,
    57, 73
Li-Fraumeni syndrome, 84, 103
Lignac, George, 94
Lissauer, Heinrich, 122
LSC. *See* leukemic stem cell
lumbar puncture, 77
lymphatic system, 50–52
lymph node, 50, 76–77, 118
lymphocytes, 47
lymphoid stem cell, 41
lymphoma, 86

M

macrophage, 43, 47, 62
magnetic fields, 84
maintenance therapy, 85
malignant tumor, 14
Manhattan Project, 89
maternal exposure to risk factors, 79–81

McCulloch, Ernest, 52
McGriffin, Jim, 52
median age, 62, 64
medical technologists, 118
megakaryocytes, 41, 44
melanoma, 24
meningioma, 86
metastasis, 14, 15
microscope, electron, 99
monocyte lineage, 43, 62
Morgagni, Giovanni Battista, 30–31
mucous membranes, 123
muscular tissues, 27
mutations of proto-oncogenes, 14
myelodysplastic syndrome, 132
myeloid stem cell, 41, 53
myeloma cell, 52
Mylotarg (gemtuzumab ozogamicin),
    124, 125

N

Nagasaki, Japan, 90
nasopharyngeal cancer, 24, 25
National Cancer Act, 7
National Cancer Institute (NCI), 7, 83, 130
National Institutes of Health (NIH), 77
National Marrow Donor Program, 73,
    117–118, 129
natural killer cell (NK cell), 43
nausea, 85, 116, 124
NCI. *See* National Cancer Institute
Neumann, Ernst, 56–57
neural tissues, 27
neutrophil, 41
NIH. *See* National Institutes of Health
Nixon, Richard, 7
NK cell. *See* natural killer cell
non-ablative allogenic stem cell
    transplantation, 132
Nowell, Peter, 67, 110–113
nucleus, 13

O

Ommaya reservoir, 124
oncogenes, 14, 104–106, 107, 115
oncogenic virus, 98
oncologist, 25
The Origin of Malignant Tumors
    (Boveri), 110
oxygen, 43

P

Paget, Stephen, 68–69
pancreas, 103
Pappenheim, Arthur, 51
pathology, 18
pentostatin, 132
pernicious anemia, 82
pesticides, 71, 84, 88, 95, 97, 101
p53. See tumor suppressor genes, *p53*
phagocytic cell, 47
phenoxy, 61
Philadelphia chromosome. *See* chromo-
    somes, Philadelphia chromosome
placenta, 76, 130
plasma, 38, 39, 40
platelets, 17, 38, 39, 44–45, 47, 48, 52–53
pluripotent stem cell, 41, 53
Potts, Percival, 34
prognosis of leukemia, 57
proliferation of blood cells, 22
protein, 13, 16, 68
proto-oncogenes, 13–14, 105, 107, 115
psoriasis, 123

R

race and leukemia, 22, 60–61
radiation
    exposure to, 23, 34, 58, 64, 69, 71,
        81, 88, 90–91, 93, 101, 104, 133
    therapy, 85, 116, 120, 121, 132
Ramayana, 24–25
receptor, 13–14
rectum, cancer of, 25
red blood cells. *See* erythrocytes
relapse, 117
remission, rates, 64, 87
retrovirus, 100
Revlimid, 132
Roman empire, 25
Rosenberg, Steven A., 130–131
Rous, Peyton, 97–98, 104
Rous sarcoma virus (RSV), 97, 104–105
Royal Infirmary (Scotland), 54
RSV. *See* Rous sarcoma virus
Rutgers University, 118

S

sarcoma, 86
Schwachman-diamond syndrome, 103
scrotal cancer, 34

Seats and Causes of Disease Investigated by Means of Anatomy (Morgagni), 31
secondary cancer. *See* cancer, secondary cancer
Sedgwick, Mr., 18
seed and soil hypothesis, 68–69
Shope papilloma virus, 98
signal molecules, 105
skin cancer, 24, 25
Sklodowska, Marie. *See* Curie, Marie
smoking, 8, 23, 34, 35, 64, 133
Sorbonne University, 92
Spiroptera carcinoma, 98–99
spleen, 17, 37, 50, 55, 76, 118
src (oncogene), 104–105
stem cells, 38, 41. *See also* leukemic stem cell
    transplantation, 85, 116, 120, 125–131, 132, 134
stomach cancer, 25
Stroud, Jennifer, 72–73
sun, overexposure to, 8
survival rates, 11, 20–22
symptoms
    of childhood leukemia, 71, 74, 76, 87
    of leukemia, 11, 17–19, 38, 57

T

therapeutic radiation, 64
therapy. *See* treatment
tissues, 13, 27
T lymphocytes, 43
tobacco. *See* smoking
tonsils, 50
topoisomerese II, 81
trachea, 76
transcription factor, 62
transformation, proto-oncogenes to oncogenes, 105, 107
translocation events, 113
trastuzuma. *See* Herceptin
treatment. *See also* bone marrow, transplant; chemotherapy; differentiation therapy; radiation, therapy; stem cells, transplantation
    for cancer, 7, 8
    for childhood leukemia, 84–87
    future, 116, 132–133, 134
    for leukemia, 20, 61, 62, 120–131
    side effects, 85–86, 87

tretinoin. *See* Vesanoid
Trisenox, 123
tropical anemia, 82
Truman, Harry, 89
tumor, 13, 14, 86
tumor suppressor genes, 13, 102, 106–108
    INK4, 108
    p53, 108, 109, 114
turmeric, 80
typhus fever, 32–33
tyrosine kinase, 68

U

umbilical cord, 129
Uniformed Services University of Health Services, 130
United States Naval Radiological Defense Laboratory, 112
University College London, 109
University of Berlin, 33
University of Dundee, 109
University of Edinburgh, 19
University of Königsberg, 56–57
University of Padua, 31
University of Pennsylvania, 112
University of Washington, 130

V

vaccine, cancer, 132
Velpeau, Alfred, 35
Vesanoid (tretinoin), 124, 125
"viral RNA," 101
Virchow, Rudolf, 27, 32–33, 37, 48, 51, 56
virus, 35
volatile solvents, 97
vomiting, side effect of treatment, 85

W

Waldeyer, Wilhelm, 32–33
Washington, George, 20–21
Wesleyan University, 112
white blood cells. *See* leukocytes
Wilms' tumor, 83
World War II, 88–90

X

X-rays, 34

ABOUT THE AUTHOR

♦

DONNA M. BOZZONE earned her B.S. in biology from Manhattan College in 1978 and her M.A. and Ph.D. in biology from Princeton University in 1980 and 1983, respectively. She continued her education as a postdoctoral research associate at the Worcester Foundation for Experimental Biology. She joined the faculty of Saint Michael's College in 1987 and is now Professor of Biology.

Dr. Bozzone's areas of specialization are in developmental and cellular biology. She teaches or has taught courses in introductory biology, science writing, cell biology, developmental biology, genetics, plant developmental physiology, and a senior seminar on the history of biology. She is the recipient of the Joanne Rathgeb Teaching Award from Saint Michael's College. An author of more than 25 publications, Dr. Bozzone is also a member of the Publication Review Panel for the *Journal of College Science Teaching* and an *ad hoc* reviewer for *American Biology Teacher*. An enthusiast for science education at all levels, Dr. Bozzone designs laboratory teaching materials for students in high school and college, and also works with students who are training to become biology teachers. She and her husband, Douglas Green, who is also a biology professor at Saint Michael's, live in Vermont with their two teenage daughters.